THE WOMAN'S BOOK OF DREAMS

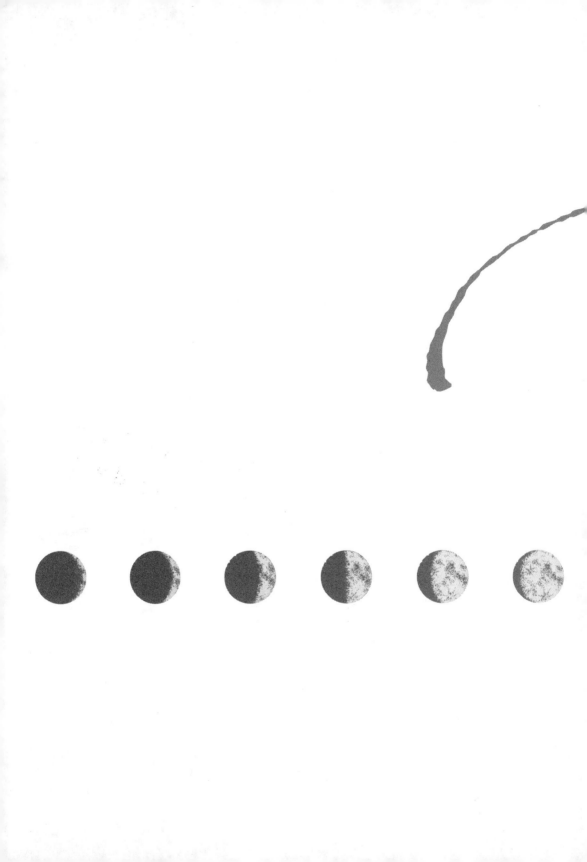

THE WOMAN'S BOOK OF

Dreams

Dreaming as a Spiritual Practice

CONNIE COCKRELL KAPLAN

BEYOND WORDS *Publishing* INC

Beyond Words Publishing, Inc.
20827 N.W. Cornell Road, Suite 500
Hillsboro, Oregon 97124-9808
503-531-8700
1-800-284-9673

Editor: Melissa Thompson
Proofreader: Marvin Moore
Design: Laura Shaw
Managing editor: Kathy Matthews
Composition: William H. Brunson Typography Services

Printed in the United States of America
Distributed to the book trade by Publishers Group West

Library of Congress Cataloging-in-Publication Data
Kaplan, Connie Cockrell, 1948–
    The woman's book of dreams : dreaming as a spiritual practice /
Connie Cockrell Kaplan.
       p.   cm.
    ISBN 1-58270-008-7 (pbk.)
    1. Women's dreams.   I. Title.
BF1099.W65K36   1999
135'.3—dc21   98-50197
                                                                            CIP

The corporate mission of Beyond Words Publishing, Inc.:
   Inspire to Integrity

This book is dedicated to Vic Kaplan.

Thank you for making my dreams come true.

In memoriam:

To Freya Bame Arthur

My dreaming sister

My sacred friend

I used to believe that I lived my life
while awake and that during sleep my psyche
presented pictures to help me understand my life.
If I broke the pictures, or dream, into small
parts (symbols) and analyzed them, I would
come to a deeper understanding of my
personal process and history.

Now I know that looking at dreaming from
the opposite direction is my life's work. Dreaming
gives us the images and vibrations
of the Dream Weave—options
ready to take form.

Dreaming gives us the future.

CONTENTS

FOREWORD

*I*was deeply honored when I was asked to write a foreword to *The Woman's Book of Dreams* and to introduce its author to the reading public, because Connie Kaplan is my friend and I have such deep respect for her work. For years, I have watched Connie as she has walked her spiritual path, and I have reveled in the beauty of the unfolding of her journey. We have shared her dreams, the profound spiritual information she has received, and we have been blessed by the tools for human growth potential brought to her by spirit. In the process, I have noted the impeccability and integrity with which she has used those tools to master each challenge that has appeared along her path.

Many of the people reading this book may not know Connie or her work because she has interacted with small groups and has kept her traveling to a minimum. Those of you in this category are in for a delightful surprise. The powerful information and significant tools that Connie has shared in this book will show you that she is not a stranger and definitely not a novice, but rather, an adept sister who has shared the path with you and who has dreamed it and walked it. Instead of adopting other people's concepts about dreaming or presenting unfounded beliefs of "how it is supposed to look," for years Connie has worked with hundreds of people in her dreaming circles and has intimate knowledge of the workings of the intangible world of dreams. One of the many gifts she offers is how to take the images and metaphors of the dream and to make them understandable to the Western mind. The cycles and seasons, rhymes and reasons for our journeys into the dreamtime are explained in this book.

Connie has approached the realm of dreams with ultimate sensitivity and has worked diligently to prepare a system that will not only offer guidelines and fuller understanding but will richly enhance the dreamer's journey by teaching how to apply the spiritual substance found in the dreaming state to life. Connie has given us a way to access deep soul memories and to rekindle our spirit's purpose for being.

The time of the remembering is upon us. Every human being is being asked to remember who they are, why they are here, and what qualities and acts of service they can offer humanity that will assist us in healing ourselves and our world. If humankind is to successfully embrace a future that nurtures all life-forms, women can no longer absolve themselves from accepting the truth. Among humans, all things are born through the feminine gender of our species. Unless women envision and dream a future that supports the forthcoming generations' right to experience life abundant, that reality will not come into manifestation. We are being asked to remember that we give birth to the future through becoming visionaries and through the spiritual discipline of dreaming.

For centuries, indigenous peoples have had secret dreaming societies that have served as guidance systems for entire civilizations during difficult times. These dreaming societies have opened the boundaries to their dreaming spaces in the past three years to include other cultures and races. The profound truths that have long been held in secret are available to any human being who embraces the discipline. Connie received the

OK from her spiritual guidance to reveal the information contained in her book during the exact time that the unfettered energy of the ancient dreamers was being released to humankind. I consider this book and all of Connie's work to be based on her hard-earned lessons and the rewards of her rich wisdom garnered along the way. Her words are gifts to each of us and to humanity. I personally feel that the tools for self-empowerment herein are a bridge that will allow each dreamer to awaken to her potential and to blossom in ways she never imagined before.

May this book and Connie's work be a blessing that will enrich the lives of every person it touches. The circle of life embraces us all, and each of us dreams that circle eternally—just as we are being dreamed by the Maker of All Things. Knowing that truth in our hearts is the remembering. Enjoy—in joy!

Jamie Sams

ACKNOWLEDGMENTS

This is a brief and certainly incomplete list of people to whom I give immeasurable thanks:

To Vic Kaplan, for teaching me about divine partnership.

To Sara Kaplan, for initiating me into motherlove.

To Ben Kaplan, for being a dream-come-true son.

To Lauren Kaplan, for teaching me about compassion.

To Nila Meriwether, my mother, for giving me the gift of dreaming.

To Marsha Hartos, for helping me clarify my words.

To Nancy Jackson, for a lifetime of loving support and kindness.

To Blanca Valencia, for loving me and my family.

To Bonnie Solow, for dedication to right livelihood and deep commitment.

To Cindy Black, for consistently expressing life in honesty and integrity.

To Richard Cohn, for swimming with the dolphins.

To Lisa Weyth Kirk, for enthusiasm.

To Julie Fox, for teaching me about dying.

To those whose dreams made this book meaningful: Carol Aronowsky, Jeanne Dancs Arthur, Beth Botansky, Tommie Cooper, Peggy Croghan, Judy Epstein, Elaine Fresco, Holiday Jackson, Sharon Jeffers, Elaine Levi, Kris McCallister, Lynn

Mitchell, Melissa Mullin, Madeleine Randall, Susan Rose, Laura Orenstein Roveda, and Evette Weyers.

To other dreamers who support this work in innumerable ways: Sara Charno, Dionna Cordova, Peggy Dunn, Amy Elliott, Marci Fabrici, Ellie Farbstein, Monique Fay, Tamar Frankiel, Judy Greenfeld, Jill Jackson, Debby Jameson, Gunnar Keel, Sydney Kopeikin, Ramona Lampell, Kathy Lander, Barbara Meyer, Iris Moskowitz, Rone Prinz, Toby Sperber, Ruth Stiles, LaKata Hasie Sweeney, Ronit Weintraub, and Wayne Wolf.

To my publishing team, for dedicated attention to this book: Cammie Doty, Pat Maple, Kathy Matthews, Marvin Moore, Karolyn Nearing (for her beautiful handwriting), Laura Shaw, Heather Speight, and Melissa Thompson.

A Dreaming Woman's Story

When I was a toddler, we moved to a house with a garden. I loved the garden, especially the strawberries, which I ate voraciously. I had many long talks with the strawberry spirits. I noticed that no one else ever talked to the spirits, so I never mentioned them to my family. The spirits' greeting and good-bye to me was always "Remember to remember." I trusted the strawberry spirits and told them everything. I tried hard to remember what they wanted me to remember.

One day the neighbor's pet monkey got loose. Like me, the monkey also loved my strawberry patch, but unlike me, he did not have respect for the patch. He destroyed the strawberries. When I went out to assess the damage, the plants were shredded, and the spirits were gone. I never returned to the patch. I felt betrayed and questioned whether the strawberry spirits ever existed. They had seemed so real and their words had seemed like truth. The admonition "Remember to remember" had been so important. But now they were gone, and except in dreams, I never saw them again.

I became obsessed with the idea that there was something I needed to remember, but I couldn't remember what. Maybe if I remembered, the strawberry spirits would come back.

Later in life, I learned that my sister Nancy had a secret relationship with the rock people in the backyard when she was a little girl! It was astonishing to know that both of us had these childhood deva friends, yet both of us were afraid to talk about them. If I had shared my strawberry spirits with my sister, I might not have experienced their disappearance as betrayal.

DREAM TEACHERS

As I grew older, I discovered that the nature spirits did not really leave me. They followed me in many forms through my dreams. When I began to pay close attention to my dreams, I noticed that recurring spirits of all kinds appeared to me with teachings.

I began having dreams of a grandfather. He was old, wore a red headband, and had a great sense of humor. He was thin, short, and wiry. He taught me how to run in the desert at night without tripping, how to chase rabbits (and catch them), and how to move up and down mountains without falling.

Also, I met a nature-spirit teacher, the delightful and ever faithful Prairie Dancer. I had gone to Montana one June to work with a Native American medicine woman. One day as I took a walk I heard a very strange sound coming from a hole in the ground. I stopped to listen.

PRAIRIE DANCER

A loud scream came from a hole in the ground. I knelt down, put my face up to the hole, and peered in. I heard a louder, more piercing scream. Suddenly, a nature spirit jumped out of the hole. The spirit said she'd screamed to test me—to see if I could hear her. She told me she was shocked I could see her. She hadn't been seen in 150 years. She was brown green with elk hips and legs and hooves. She told me her name was Prairie Dancer.

Prairie Dancer became my friend. She told me that the strawberry spirits of my childhood were probably terrorized by the monkey and just hiding. If I had gone back a few days later, the spirits would have been there. Prairie Dancer told me that if I went home and planted a prairie in my yard, she would come and live with me. I planted and she came. She is still visible in my front yard, especially during the magic hour around twilight.

DREAMING MYSELF AWAKE

I knew that dream teachers held the keys to my life, but at that time, I still had respect for the unwritten social rules: a woman must not shine too brightly, must not be too bright, and must not ask any questions not easily answered by a man. Social rules also taught me that a woman must always question her sanity. Somehow I knew that dreaming was a woman's realm, but I seriously wondered whether anyone else on the planet knew. I spoke rarely about my dreams. However, I learned from them.

When I was thirty-six years old, I was living an enviable life. I had a successful career as an associate director in television. I had a great husband and a beautiful family, and life was good. Then suddenly I got sick. I encountered a virus that rendered me incapable of working. While the illness was primarily physical, it affected my mind most profoundly. I lost big pieces of my memory. I lost the ability to sort information. I lost the mind that had served me so well in my early adult life. For eighteen months, I did little else but sleep. Therefore, I did little else but dream.

During that powerful dreaming time, the inner teachers changed somewhat. They became very pedantic. They came, they taught me specific things to do with dreaming, and they gave me specific techniques and pieces of information. For eighteen months, I was in dream school! And during that time, I dreamed myself awake.

Through my dream teachers, I learned what I was to remember: I now understand that truth presents itself in dreaming and later exposes itself in form. The dreamer must simply learn to read the signs and track the energy. The spirituality I experienced in waking life during childhood had carried through to my adulthood in dreams.

I learned through these dreams that truth is not a noun but a dimension—a dreaming dimension. In the dimension of truth, one is in direct relationship with energy without the restraints of personal will or social laws. The need for things to make sense no longer exists. Truth is boundless. The opposite of truth is not "lie" but rather a sense of separation—the sense I had when I lost the strawberry spirits. Truth does not exist in the realm of language. Real truth exists in one's ability to move into its dimension. This book will help you—the reader/dreamer—do just that.

MY GIFT TO YOU

The first part of this book provides more of my story as a dreaming woman. I think it is important for dreamers everywhere to remember and share their stories. I hope that through hearing and understanding my story, your own will come to light. As I began to remember myself as a dreamer, I began to "remember" my authentic self and my life's work. I hope that you will have the same experience! The first part of the book also outlines techniques I have learned from dream teachers in dreamtime. It describes how the moon affects your dreaming and the types of dreaming you may have under certain lunar circumstances. You will learn who you are as a dreamer and how to track and chart your own dreaming patterns.

The second part of the book introduces the life-changing form called *dream circle*. This section presents a structure that helps you use dreaming as a tool to enrich your life. My dream circles are similar to ancient women's circles. Over the years, however, new aspects have been integrated. In this section of the book, dream circle is outlined for you.

The information in the third and fourth parts documents the results of my circles. I have gathered dreams, personal testimony of the dreamers, and life experiences to show you how dream circle can change your life.

This book is unusual to read (as it was to write) because dreaming cannot be spoken directly, nor can it be defined consummately. Dreaming can only be spoken indirectly—in metaphor. Nothing is precise about dreaming, yet to be a dreamer, one must be extraordinarily precise in living the dream.

This book is for the dreamer in every reader. It speaks to one who knows and joyfully embraces the mystery of metaphor. The reader must alter her consciousness to read the book. She must read with the eyes of the womb—cyclical eyes, the eyes of dreaming. The book describes a personal *and* collective process that cannot be seen or touched, but it can be validated. The reader has to test the information against her knowingness and then interact with the book accordingly. My book was written to stir ancient memories in you.

PART ONE

HOW THESE TEACHINGS
CAME TO BE

Dream Lines

In the beginning was the dream. Through the dream all things were made, and without the dream nothing was made that has been made.

THOMAS BERRY
The Dream of the Earth

HONORING THE MOON TIME

*I*t was early January when I made my first trek to meet Minisa Crumbo-Halsey, a Creek-Potawatomi medicine woman living in the hills above Malibu. The day was crisp and cold—Southern California cold: the sun was warm but the air was chilly. The road was winding and unfamiliar. I felt like I was truly on a medicine journey. I had butterfly stomach and sensed I would never be the same after this meeting. I was right.

Minisa asked me to sit on the ground. We were high on a hill overlooking the Pacific Ocean. She bent me into a position so miserably uncomfortable that my body dominated my attention and screamed for relief. I stayed in the position because I knew that my body's pain was making my mind take a back seat. What Minisa had to say must bypass the mind.

Minisa reminded me of the sacred connection between a woman and the moon; a woman's very life depends on the moon's pull over her body. She explained how the moon controls a woman's cycles just as surely as it controls the ocean's tides. She told me that the ocean is Mother Earth's cyclical waters and that menstrual blood is mine. My body remembered that it was from the earth. That day, the earth became my mother, and I understood my body as a mini version of her.

The following paragraphs are my journal entry from that day—my memory of what Minisa said after I digested it, drove home, and wrote it down:

THE WOMEN'S TEACHINGS

Women are life givers. Men are life makers. Women dream the dream and give the gift. Men manifest and focus the dream.

As women, it is our sacred charge to purify and re-dream the world. We are responsible for dreaming the dream made manifest in waking reality. In the white man's world, we believe we dream about our waking life at night, and through dreams, we gain an understanding. This is backwards. In women's teachings, first we dream the dream, then we bring the dream into manifestation, and then comes understanding.

Since we are responsible for the dream, it is our most sacred duty to free ourselves from any blocks to our visions. Emotions held in our bodies block dreaming and prevent us from owning our power. A sacred and timeless woman's belief teaches that a periodic cleansing is the way to honor our power and meet our responsibilities to the universe.

Our bodies are micro-universes: bodies have the seven stars of the Pleiades (chakras), the planets (organs), and moons.

Women's ovaries make little moons. When each little moon is released into the system, women give the universe their bodies' creative power. As the little moon makes its way through the tubes, it does not know its destiny. The little moon is simply all potential: it has no wants or needs. This is a time of all possibility for women.

The key to honoring our woman power is pledging to become the dreaming women we came here to be. Make the pledge to be that woman, and begin honoring your moon time.

Though I had never heard Minisa's words before, they stirred an ancient memory in me. These words were part of the strawberry spirits' imperative, "Remember to remember."

THE DREAMING LINES

Not long after my meeting with Minisa, I sat in ceremony with some friends. The experience I had that night changed my life and seeded the information of this book. The following is an entry from my journal. This particular experience was essential to the development of my dream work.

Dream Lines

Last night at a ceremony, a medicine woman used a deer rattle to send each participant into an altered consciousness. By the time she came to me (I was the sixteenth person), I was already deep in trance.

I knelt down. The medicine woman began rattling. I felt crackling and popping in my spine. The rattle sounded like crystals on the floor of a cave.

Suddenly I saw that women have points of light circling their wombs. The points extend into gossamer lines that connect with the moon. As the moon moves through the signs of the zodiac, it plucks the light lines like harp strings. This action awakens a specific dreaming vibration in the dreamer's womb and determines the type of dreaming she will have on a particular night

THE WOMB IS THE DREAMING ORGAN

My "vision" was unusual because it was also a mental experience. I "saw" the lines shooting out of women's wombs. I simultaneously felt the lines emanating from my womb. I "dream knew" what the lines were and how they had worked for ever and always. Memories seemed to be pouring forth from some very ancient women's tradition. I felt that I had been temporarily thrown back to a Neolithic village temple, and the training reconstructed itself in my awareness. The memories may sound familiar to you, too.

The womb is the dreaming organ. Dreaming comes to us through the internal, secret knowledge of the womb. There are incredibly subtle energies connected to a woman's womb that she does not necessarily understand unless she goes through very exhaustive training with a female shaman or sorcerer. Just as a woman who gives birth to a child does not know the biological processes in the womb that create those perfect toes, fingers, and a precious little nose, neither does she fully understand the subtle spiritual dreaming energy connected to the organ.

The relationship between the womb and the moon controls every aspect of dreaming. A woman's cycles and her dreaming are inextricable. Even women who have had hysterectomies, or for any other reason no longer bleed, still have the cyclical relationship to the moon and the light lines connected to her. The moon moves across the sky and interfaces with an invisible force field called the Dream Weave. The Dream Weave is known to all indigenous peoples. It is the invisible pattern of connection that links human thought to form, and possibility to awareness. Physicist Fritjof Capra calls it the web of life consisting of networks within networks of increasing possibility. The gossamer lines connected to each dreamer also connect to the Weave. The moon, which is a part of the Weave, sends specific types of dream information into the womb of the dreamer. The information sent depends on where the moon sits in the heavens that night.

Interestingly, a menopausal woman's lines of light disconnect from the moon and reconnect to the sun (hot flashes). Her relationship with fire becomes stronger, and in many ways, her dreaming becomes more sophisticated. Yet her dreaming still relates to lunar cycles, and she still recognizes her dream patterns in the same way as before menopause.

You may wonder about male dreamers. I have not seen the lines of light coming from a man, but some males' dreams convince me that some men dream like women dreamers. Men also have lunar cycles, and certainly those cycles are energetically traceable. Each gender has specialized energies that create preferences for certain kinds of life experiences. Both men and women have potential for and access to all the energies of the universe, but both men and women have specific dominant traits. Men, of course, can be just as powerful in their dreaming as women. However, my dream circles and I have found that men's dreams tend to be more concrete and personal. Men, for example, often have great power to encounter personal aspects of themselves or to reach deeper understandings of their abilities in dreaming. Women's dreams are often more relational and collective. Women have a stronger sense that the womb is the source of all life, whereas men, not having wombs, are more connected to their own individual lives. It is more difficult for men to imagine that their dreaming is connected to the universe.

The womb is the door of birth, the door of creation, the door of a dreamer's energy. By perfecting the use of the womb's creative energy, one becomes ecstatically alive; one perfects the ability to love and to dream.

WHAT IS A DREAM?

I define *dreaming* as a direct encounter with energy in the dimension of truth. *Dreaming may occur in both waking and sleeping consciousness.* A dream exists beyond language. By the time you put words and descriptions on a dream, you are already several generations removed from the actual experience. The experience of a dream is primal and incomparable. It is pre-verbal and presensual.

This definition of dreaming combines both indigenous teachings and the understanding I have gained directly through dreams. It expands the scientific rapid eye movement definitions but certainly does not contradict them.

Let me explain further. When we first go to sleep, our consciousness moves on the lines of light extending from our wombs into a void space. In those moments, there is no sense of ego or personality, no thinking or feeling. Our personal will relaxes. We experience a period of complete rest in the familiar blackness. During this time, the dreamer floats freely in consciousness. She is in direct relationship with all potential energy and in direct relationship with her own soul purpose—the reason she exists. *This is the dream.* We all reach the dream state automatically as we drift toward deep sleep.

For a while, the dreamer stays in this comfortable, all-nourishing blackness. During this time, the physical body is regenerated. Soon, though, the energy of the dreamer strengthens, and the rested dreamer magnetizes a specific experience—something she needs to "remember" about her soul's intent. This is the dream—this deep energetic connection to her soul.

When the energetic experience becomes definable, the mental body of the dreamer "awakens" within dreamscape and begins assigning meaning to the experience. It is the mind's responsibility to make sense of things, after all, and the freshly rejuvenated mind of the dreamer is ready for action. The mind pulls from a giant lexicon of personal and collective symbols to make a story line representing the energetic experience so the dreamer can (hopefully) remember. This is when the eyes start wiggling and rapid eye movement sleep occurs.

Ideally, the dreamer awakens into ordinary consciousness out of the dream experience, remembers the story line, and uses the information in daily reality.

Every time we return to ordinary consciousness from dreaming, we awaken changed. Through dreams, we encounter new information from the dimension of truth. We can choose whether—and how—to integrate that change into everyday life. We can opt to return to yesterday's limited understanding of the world, or we can move into today's expanded understanding. We can choose to be exhilarated and augmented by a dream, or we can dismiss it as "just a dream."

Whatever our choice, we have traveled on the dream lines, we have received the influence of the moon, and we have changed. Each time we awaken, we awaken to new possibility. The dreamer's free will and personal integrity determine how the dream will be manifested.

GREAT DREAMER AND THE DREAM WEAVE

As we dream, we are also being dreamed by an unfathomable intelligence. This concept is the crux of understanding dreaming. Whether one calls this intelligence Great Dreamer, God, Universal Mind, Great Spirit—or Bernie, for that matter—every dreamer must realize that she is being dreamed by a larger, more omniscient energy than herself. I personalize this omniscient energy as Great Dreamer, because it makes the experience of being dreamed richer for me. Great Dreamer is the matrix of the universe that holds creation. The matrix is the *invisible force*, the Spirit, that motivates creation and evokes evolution. We are indeed governed and nourished by the unseen as well as the seen. If I can understand myself as an extension of that matrix, I can then begin to remember who I am in the story of creation.

There are dreamers from all dimensions of this universe. All sentient beings dream. We human earth dreamers are partners with other dreaming beings. We are all dreaming together. We are all creating the Great Dream, the universal consensus. We all meet in dreamtime on the dimension of truth. Together, we are co-creating the potentials that exist within the laws of truth. Great Dreamer simultaneously feeds us dream information and receives our dreams. She and we are a part of the wholeness of the universe.

All sentient beings have their own layer of consciousness— their own spectrum of perception. The overlay and interfacing of those spectra create the Dream Weave. A single species or single layer of sentience cannot perceive the totality of creation. That is Great Dreamer's job.

Collective dreaming creates a tapestry of possibility. When we join other dreamers, both of this planet and of the cosmos, we build a consensus for reality. This consensus is the unseen pattern ultimately governing form. This pattern is the Dream Weave. I sometimes visualize the Dream Weave as a giant invisible jungle gym stretching multidimensionally throughout the galaxies of the universes. The Dream Weave holds all possibilities. It is the infrastructure where all laws—cosmic, galactic, physical, and natural—begin. The Dream Weave is truth flowing through space-time.

Picture children at play choosing various bars from which to hang as they scamper across a jungle gym. When a child's hand grabs a bar, picture the bar lighting up and coming to life with color. This is how I see dreamers selecting various threads on the Weave as they dream potential into manifestation. When a dreamer grabs onto a possibility, she gives it life, awakens it, enlightens it, densifies it, and dreams the potential toward manifestation.

We dream our world into being by playing on the Dream Weave—selecting potentialities existing in the infrastructure of the Weave and pulling them toward life. We interweave our gossamer lines with the lines of other dreamers and create a blueprint for all possibility.

Our governments change, because we dream them to change. The Berlin Wall came down, because we dreamed it down. Apartheid ended, because we dreamed it away. Changes occurring in dreams are literal and very real.

Simultaneously, we are being dreamed. As we make choices for life and peace on our planet, Great Dreamer dreams us toward life and peace. Conversely, if we make non-beneficial choices in dreaming, Great Dreamer assists us in experiencing the consequences of our choices. When we play on the invisible jungle gym, we receive a nurturing life force. Dreaming enlivens us.

Goethe informed us of how life works when he said, "The moment one definitely commits oneself, then Providence moves, too. All sorts of things occur to help one that would never otherwise have occurred." When we dream the dream and commit to it, Great Dreamer moves enormous forces to manifest the dream.

Scientific research concludes that dreaming is a necessary part of living, although most scientists admit they do not know why. I suggest that this is because scientists ignore the opposite side of dreaming: *being dreamed*. My experience is that the dream dreams me as surely as I dream the dream. The dream feeds me. The interdependence of the dreamer and the dream is inseparable. One must deeply understand the interrelationship to truly understand dreaming.

The first thing a dreamer knows is that she is being dreamed. She understands herself as a vital part of a great wholeness that empowers her as a creative being. When the dreamer knows this, she is on her way to mastery. The dreamer literally falls in love with herself and with all life. The dreamer trusts herself and her dreaming. She becomes the embodiment of the Weave.

THE VESSEL

The womb is the dream vessel. The moon sends dream food in the form of images in dreamtime. The dreamer contains the images and holds the juice. The dreamer is the chalice.

When working on a potter's wheel, one uses resistance to build a vessel. One must know how to surrender to the clay, yet at the same time one must know how to evoke the shape. One senses what the clay wants to do, yet one finds the centering place that makes the clay's form aesthetic and useful. Similarly, as dreamers, we have to surrender to the Great Dream, but we also have to ruthlessly create ourselves as the vessel that contains the Great Dream. If the vessel is weak, it will not hold the dream.

We must be strong and clear vessels. When we know our cycles and patterns, we can learn to be intentional vessels. We can learn to dream into manifestation a reality that benefits all living creatures, the planet, and the universe. The goal of all dreamers is to co-create a life that is in alignment with the soul's divine plan.

We are both the pot and the potter. We are the container for the dream fluid, and we give form to the dream material that comes our way. Some of us write the dream material down or speak it at dream circle. Some of us act the dream material out through our lives—our art, parenting, or careers.

I have found that using a "dream bowl" is a profound way, both metaphorically and concretely, to enhance dreaming.

Dream Bowl

Connie

A teacher came to me and asked me to bring her the "dream bowl." I saw a terra-cotta bowl about the size of two hands with a midnight blue interior and crystals in the four directions. I could see energy swirling into the bowl. I found a blue feather that I knew was to hang off the bowl's north crystal. I tried to wake up holding the feather, but I dropped it when the phone awakened me.

This dream came long before my first pottery class. I tried to make the bowl with modeling clay from a children's hobby store but was highly disappointed with my results. Fortunately, a few weeks later, I found and bought a bowl that worked with some moderate revisions. I put the bowl by my head when I went to sleep. I began to see clearer colors and sharper images in my dreams. Since then, I have made dream bowls for other dreamers. The bowls have amazingly helped people contain and remember their dreams. Dream bowls serve as external reminders of who we are.

We are the chalice, the earthen cup. Our wombs are the bowls into which the dream images pour. We are the vessels of the dream. Our gossamer lines of light deliver images to us. We contain the images, bring them to life, and give birth to them. This is the nature of dreaming.

2

Astrology and
the Dream

*Neptune sings: "Through my vivid and infinitely creative imagination, I am
constantly co-creating with the divine the myriad richness of life's possibilities.
I am dreaming the universe into being."*

CAROLINE W. CASEY
Making the Gods Work for You

The woman's womb, the vessel of the dream, fills with
images during a dream or a visionary experience. The
astrological conditions of the moon determine the
nature of those images. To understand and explore dreaming,
one must know a little about astrology.

In this chapter, I will outline the basic astrological information that affects dreaming. Read the information and use it
as a guideline, a resource, or a springboard. If you want to
explore astrology further, or if you already know more than a
little about astrology and care to expand on the concept, it is
yours to do!

DREAMTIME AND THE
SOUL CONTRACT

When a person is born, she brings with her certain energetic gifts. She brings these gifts from her soul and delivers them through her dreams and actions to humanity and to Earth herself. A dreamer "seals" her contract with life at the moment of birth. In that contract, her gifts are delineated. Destiny crystallizes at that moment, and the journey of the gift bearer begins. However, she almost immediately forgets the contract! A good portion of her life is spent trying to remember.

One way to read the contract is through an astrological chart. From the dreamer's perspective, each planet's placement in the chart represents a clause in the soul contract. Dreaming is a technique we use to check in with our soul and revisit our contract on a regular basis. Through dreams, the soul reminds dreamers of the gifts they bear. It does not, however, tell dreamers how evolved they are and therefore how gracefully they will bring their gifts to the Mother.

Your gift to Mother Earth is totally unique. To understand your gift and your soul contract, you must look for meaningful connections and patterns in your life. Dreaming is your study guide. The more conscious and aware you are of dream patterns, the more actively you participate in your destiny.

The soul contract is interesting because it is paradoxical. The contract defines your gift and destiny, yet it also allows you full authority over life. You can make all life decisions undeterred by any external force. Whatever the outcome of your decisions, the dreaming continues to reveal your contract and support you as a dreamer.

I have studied dream systems, metaphysical systems, physical systems, and spiritual systems. I have been apprenticed to

Native American shamans, African shamans, Kabbalists, mystics, and martial artists. I have sat with channelers, religious leaders, academicians, and New Agers. There is something they all have in common: they all ultimately know that the connection between spirit and matter exists in a great web of consciousness—the Dream Weave. They all teach that the true student of life learns by studying her unique role in the interrelated, interconnected, unbroken wholeness. The imperative of the dreamer is to participate in the interdependent structuring of creation's wholeness.

THE MOON CALLS US TO DREAMTIME

The moon governs our life cycles. As the moon makes her monthly trek around the zodiacal circle, she aspects (comes into relationship with) other planets. Her position each night creates an energetic dynamic that sends specific kinds of dreaming along the dream lines. Each dreamer's symbols will vary according to her relationship to the moon's position that night.

The moon, our nearest galactic neighbor, plucks our personal dream lines and evokes images that create our dreams. She holds Mother Earth in gravitational balance; she holds people in energetic balance. Stirring the ancient wisdom in each dreamer, the moon calls us to dreamtime.

THE SIGNS AND PLANETS

There are twelve astrological signs and twelve planets or zodiacal positions that the dreamer needs to know:

Symbols of the Zodiac

SIGNS	SYMBOL
Aries	♈
Taurus	♉
Gemini	♊
Cancer	♋
Leo	♌
Virgo	♍
Libra	♎
Scorpio	♏
Sagittarius	♐
Capricorn	♑
Aquarius	♒
Pisces	♓

PLANETS	SYMBOL
Sun	☉
Moon	☽
Mercury	☿
Venus	♀
Mars	♂
Jupiter	♃
Saturn	♄
Uranus	♅
Neptune	♆
Pluto	♇
Mid-heaven	MID
Ascendant	ASC

DREAMING WITH THE MOON IN THE SIGNS

The astrological signs represent how energy moves, spirals, cycles, and changes. Each sign has unique characteristics. As the moon moves through the astrological signs each month, the dream energy takes on some of the characteristics of each sign. Remember, the moon moves through all twelve signs of the zodiac every month, spending more than two but less than three days in each one. You may have an "Aries" type dream when the sun is in Cancer—because it is the *moon's* position that defines the dreaming! You'll want to buy a *Pocket Astrologer* calendar—Jim Maynard makes a very good one (Quicksilver Productions, P.O. Box 340, Ashland, Oregon 97520)—so you can check the location of the moon each night!

Be very careful, however, not to become literal with the information of this chapter. Each dreamer's contract is unique. Your relationship to each sign is totally yours. Some signs may be more powerfully placed in your astrological chart than others. This section is a study guide, not a dictionary or a rule book.

What follows is a broad-strokes summary of the energy you may experience in dreaming when the moon moves through the zodiac. The energies will vary according to the season, the sun's placement, other planets, and your own lunar cycle every month. These are simply guidelines to begin your personal investigations.

Aries Dreaming

Aries is the first sign of the zodiac and the initiation of a new cycle. In the yearly calendar, Aries begins on the first day of spring—the vernal equinox. When the moon is in Aries, dreams may be about new beginnings, new rules, new limits to test, or new understandings of old ideas. Aries dreams reveal the dreamer's new relationship to ancient cycles. The "mascot" of Aries is the ram—he who bangs his head. Aries dreams, therefore, may be about the head: headaches, new ways of thinking, or a new focus.

Taurus Dreaming

Taurus is a very earthy, sensual sign. Taurus loves beauty and loves to nurture nature. When the moon is in Taurus, dreams might be about stewardship of Mother Earth. Taurus dreams might also involve different kinds of nurturing: caretaking, tending, cooking, gardening, and land loving. The Taurus mascot is the bull. Taurus rarely takes no for an answer! So, Taurus dreams may include a certain bullish, determined, sturdy, and enduring energy, and the dreams may be about accomplishment against odds. Taurus also governs the throat, so some dreams may refer to singing or speaking—using voice to bring beauty to the planet.

Gemini Dreaming

Gemini is the twin sign. Geminis can see the connectedness of all things. Mirror dreams often appear when the moon is in Gemini, because Geminis see form as a mirror. This sign also governs the lungs, so dreams of breath may occur. Gemini dreams may illuminate the principle of reciprocity: giving and receiving energy, the metaphorical breath. Geminis love to learn. They appreciate ideas for their own sake, and they are good at acquiring knowledge. The moon may send information to a dreamer at this time. Library dreams and school dreams ("Oh, no, I forgot to study for the test!") may occur when the moon is in Gemini.

Cancer Dreaming

In the Northern Hemisphere, the sun moves into Cancer on the summer solstice, the longest day and shortest night of the year. It is the turning point between the dance of light and dark. Each month when the moon is in Cancer, dreams may bring forth the dreamer's personal relationship with the light and dark cosmic dance. Cancer is the home of the moon, and it is the most feminine of the signs. Often, dreams of the mother/child dynamic will come when the moon is in

Cancer. Cancer governs the womb (the dreaming organ), the ovaries, and the breasts. Regeneration and procreation may be Cancerian dream themes. Natural cycles, changing tides, changing emotions (inner tides), and water sports may be other Cancer dreams.

Leo Dreaming

Leo represents an ecstatically alive and joyous life force. Leo honors all things born of love: children, art, visions, and inspirations. Leo wants what is best for the community and loves to inspire people to be their best. Theater dreams and party dreams are most likely to occur when the moon is in Leo. The ruler of Leo is the sun, the heart chakra. As a result, dreams of one's true nature, one's innocent lust for life, come at this time. Running off to join the circus is an example of a Leo dream. The lion is Leo's symbol—king of the jungle and king of great hair! Often hair dreams and dreams of intelligence occur when the moon is in Leo. Dreams that involve actual lions also have a tendency to come when the moon aspects Leo.

Virgo Dreaming

Virgo, the virgin, is always appropriate. She is pure, polished, focused, discriminating, and a perfectionist. Some call Virgo nit-picky. Dreams of getting affairs and objects in order may come when the moon is in Virgo. Virgo has very high standards and pays great attention to detail. One might have researcher dreams, scientist dreams, analysis dreams, or critical dreams at this time. Virgo rules the intestines and the pancreas, so Virgo dreams may be about body issues. One may have dreams about breaking down and assimilating food and/or information. Virgo is also a great healing sign, so the dreamer may either receive or be taught a healing technique in Virgo dreamtime.

Libra Dreaming

Libra represents life's balancing force. Some say that Libra is the most karmic sign in the zodiac, for karma is the great balancing force. Yearly, the sun moves into Libra on the autumnal equinox, marking the beginning of winter. When the moon is in Libra, dreams may be difficult. Libra dreams may point toward unbalanced energies. They may be a road map for necessary journeys into the underworld, into the "winter" of the soul. Libra is also the sign of justice and diplomacy, so Libra dreams may inspire the dreamer to take civil action and demand justice. Libra also governs the kidneys. A Libra dream may alert one about abnormal kidney function, or the dream may point out a need for a more proper energy flow within the dreamer's life.

Scorpio Dreaming

Transformation, death, and rebirth are the anchor points of Scorpio. These words may scare some people. Dreamers, however, know that death in a dream marks a profound and exciting transformation. "Deconstruct and reconstruct" could be the motto of Scorpio. Dreams of giving birth, shedding skin (snake dreams), death, or profound change may come when the moon is in Scorpio. Scorpio is the sign of shrewd intelligence and deep insight, so dreams that come at this time may allow the dreamer to see beneath the surface. Scorpio also governs the nose. Aromatherapy dreams, anyone?

Sagittarius Dreaming

Sagittarius is the teacher's teacher. Religion, philosophy, theology, and spirituality are the favorite topics of Sagittarius. The Sagittarian tests, verifies, and easily dumps any information that does not measure up to his or her ethic. Sagittarius dreams may involve religious ceremonies, spiritual experiences, and scientific testing. Sagittarius governs the blood. Dreams may refer to the sense of inner peace invoked by proper blood flow. Sagittarius also governs the thighs, so dreams of strength and power may come at this time. Dreams of magnificent sports feats are not unusual when the moon is in Sag.

Capricorn Dreaming

Capricorn holds dominion over the forces of nature. He is the master of manifestation. In the Northern Hemisphere, the sun moves into Capricorn on the winter solstice, the shortest day and longest night of the year—which is also said to be King Arthur's birthday. Winter solstice marks another turn in the dance of light and dark. Capricorn dreams may be authoritarian and depict power over, as well as service to, nature. Capricorn rules the bones—the framework of the body. Because we download information into our bones, dreams when the moon is in Capricorn may evoke memory stored in our bones. Similarly, Mother Earth downloads information into her skeletal system—the minerals. Capricorn dreams may be crystal or stone dreams. They may call up some deep information or visualize the beauty of the mineral world. Capricorn also rules the knees. As a result, Capricorn dreams may be humbling and remind us to serve others.

Aquarius Dreaming

Aquarius is the sign of the New Age: the age of brotherhood, equanimity, and social justice. Aquarius tends to community needs and is always concerned with the group benefit. Dreams with the moon in Aquarius may be telepathic. They may allow the dreamer to perceive information from the collective consciousness. Aquarius dreams may inspire the dreamer toward social action. In addition, according to traditional astrology, Aquarius is an air sign. Dreams may depict certain properties of "air wave" communication, or they may involve air travel or wind. Tornado and tidal-wave dreams may come during an Aquarius moon.

Pisces Dreaming

Pisces, the most charitable and philanthropic sign, brings dreams that are mystical, psychic, and collective. Fluidity, unpredictability, and sensitivity are Pisces characteristics. Pisces is the sign of strong emotion and deep feeling. Pisceans love to escape. Pisces dreams can be of solitude, talking and breathing under water, deep secrecy, sacrifice, or running away. The Piscean Age, from which we now pass, was the age of great devotion to religion and organization. As a result, Pisces dreams may also reflect piety and unbending loyalty to a cause or a person.

Void-of-Course Dreaming

As the moon moves from sign to sign during a month, she may, for a few hours, be outside the direct influence of any sign. (Those constellations are far apart!) When the moon is between signs, she is said to be void of course. If you have a dream during that time, it will often be a dream of very profound quality. Usually, when the moon is void of course, nothing much happens. Women have been known to *stop labor*, wait for the moon to move into a new sign, and start again. If a dream comes when the moon is void of course, it is *important*. For example, I have received virtually *all* my dreaming information when the moon was void of course.

DREAMING WITH THE MOON ASPECTING THE PLANETS

As the moon moves around the zodiac each month, she also aspects (comes into relationship with) the planets in the sky. On the imaginary wheel called the zodiac, the moon takes a new position every few minutes. As she moves, she creates imaginary geometric angles between herself and the other planets of the solar system. The angles, traditionally, evoke specific energetic dynamics that affect everyone on earth.

In traditional astrology, the exact nature of the angle between the moon and each planet is important. In dreaming, the angle is not as important as the energetic relationship between the moon and that planet. Your *Pocket Astrologer* calendar will tell you exactly what planets the moon aspects each day.

Please do not take the following suggestions as law. They are guidelines. You may want to study them and then check to see if they are true for you. If they are not, the dream charting taught in chapter 4 will help you see why. Each dreamer is unique, and each dreamer has the right to see dreaming according to her soul contract.

PIE CHART
See page 60

COMPUTER CHART
See page 66

Sun Dreaming

A typical astrological reading usually begins with a discussion of your sun sign, because that tells you a lot about your life tendencies. Similarly, the sun clause in the soul contract tells the dreamer her principal reason for being on earth. The gift the dreamer bears from her soul is primarily defined by the sun in her chart. In traditional astrology, the sun is one's essential means of expression. Dreams that come when the moon is aspecting the sun may illuminate one's life purpose. Sun dreams may bring the dreamer closer to being radiantly and radically alive. The sun shines on all alike—wicked and righteous. And the sun is the ultimate teacher of generosity. Sun dreams may give the dreamer a deeper understanding of generosity. Each month when the moon is in the sign of the dreamer's natal sun (commonly known as your sun sign—where the sun was in the zodiac on the day of your birth), whether or not the moon is aspecting the heavenly sun, sun dreams are also likely to occur.

The sun shines of its own accord: the planets reflect the sun. For this reason, sun dreaming is very powerful. When the moon is aspecting the sun during a dream, she is reflecting the sun's energy more directly at that moment. The moon does not reflect the light of any other planet besides the sun. That makes the moon's relationship to the sun's energy stronger. Therefore, the dreaming tends to be more direct. For example, my natal sign is Sagittarius. Each month, when the moon is in Sagittarius, I always look for dreams that help illuminate my life path. On those months when the moon is in Sagittarius and is *also* aspecting the physical sun, I am especially alert.

The next three planets reflect the personal aspects of our lives: the mental body, emotional body, and physical body.

Mercury Dreaming

The decision to live on this planet includes a decision to think. We all develop a mental body. The Mercury clause in the soul contract helps the dreamer understand her unique style of thinking. Dreams when the moon is aspecting Mercury may be about the mind and help you understand your thought process. Mercury dreams may involve telepathy. They may include factual information. The Roman Mercury was the message bearer for the gods. Mercury dreams may bring important messages to you. Mercury's Greek counterpart, Hermes, was an alchemist and magician who invented the alphabet and the musical scale. As a result, Mercury dreams may be symbolic. Sanskrit, Hebrew, Egyptian, or other ancient letters may appear in Mercury dreams. Divination, magic, musical tones, or alchemical transformations may also occur during Mercury dreams.

Venus Dreaming

The emotional body is another unique pillar important to the quality of our lives. Venus, the goddess of love, represents the invisible emotional force attracting life experiences to us. Our feelings about the experiences we attract determine how joyfully we live. Dreams that come when the moon is aspecting Venus may give us very important clues about our emotional makeup. Every culture I have studied has a goddess similar to Venus who is also friendly with the snake: Lilith, Isis, Gaia, Brigid, Freyja, Xochiquetzal, and Shakti. Snake dreams often come when the moon and Venus are dancing with one another in the skies. Venus dreams are often difficult, because dreams that evoke emotion frighten us!

Mars Dreaming

Mars energy is expressed through physical activity. The Mars clause in the soul contract determines the dreamer's relationship to physical urges, personal will, volition, physical strength, and the life force animating the body. Dreams of body contact, ranging from sexual experiences to combat, may come when the moon aspects Mars. Mars energy is elemental energy. Dreams of nature spirits, plant devas, and rocks and minerals may come at this time. Because power and strength involve disintegration and resistance, those principles may come forth in Mars dreams.

Personal pillars such as the mental, emotional, and physical aspects of one's life often involve personal dreams. However, as we move farther out into the solar system, we encounter the outer planets, which move more slowly and send more universal energies to the dreamer.

Jupiter Dreaming

Jupiter has sixteen moons and is, therefore, a mini solar system. Jupiter is the god of good fortune. The Jupiter clause in the soul contract reflects how the universe supports and endorses human life. Jupiter gives meaning to life by making it valuable (good fortune). Jupiter dreams may involve shattering, for they often "break" an old pattern or smash a form so the dreamer can perceive the truth within. Jupiter energy is expansive, and as a result, the dreams may encourage the dreamer to break free. Flying dreams, liberation dreams, and dreams of impossible stunts may come when the moon aspects the big benevolent Jupiter.

Saturn Dreaming

Saturn provides walls and limitations for life on earth so that we can focus and experience the delicious specifics of life. Every person limits life differently. This means that every person experiences form differently. Dreams of responsibility or accountability may come when the moon aspects Saturn. Sometimes, Saturn dreams may feel restrictive and involve claustrophobic or constraining sensations. Other times, Saturn dreams may involve wearing tight-fitting clothes or shoes. The main thrust of Saturn dreaming, however, is to understand the consensus reality in which we live. Through Saturn dreams, we learn how our unique contributions to collective experience create that consensus.

Uranus Dreaming

Uranus, often said to be a higher-octave or more sophisticated version of Mercury, creates a lightning-bolt flash of understanding. Suddenly, at Uranus's insistence, we see ourselves authentically. Then, again as suddenly as a lightning bolt, that sight disappears. As a result, profound change often occurs. Electric-current dreams, telephone dreams, and risk-taking dreams may come when the moon aspects Uranus, or Uranus may bring an oracular dream that suddenly sheds light on a problem we have been trying to solve. The changes made in waking reality resulting from Uranus dreams will be radically enlivening. Uranus dreams jolt us into clarity and make it impossible to pretend we do not understand ourselves!

Neptune Dreaming

Neptune, the god of the sea, brings dreams of collective consciousness. Neptune, the physical planet, recently moved into the sign of Aquarius, the New Age sign, and will stay there for several years. As a result, your Neptune collective dreams may be about the whole human family, an age of peace, or a connection with other beings—many of whom we don't know in waking. Neptune dreams may also involve dreams within dreams.

In other words, you may dream that you are dreaming. Neptune reminds us of our need to dream and of our necessity to stop, stare, and feel. Neptune dreams connect us to our soul mates, or those people who we feel we know on the deepest levels.

Pluto Dreaming

Pluto is the god of the underworld. Dreams when the moon is aspecting Pluto are deep. Pluto dreams may take us on our sacred journey into the realms of the unknown. Pluto dreams may be our nightmares. However, they may also be our most sacred dreams—the ones when we go into ceremony or walk in underground labyrinths. Pluto, because of his awful reputation earned when he kidnapped the beautiful Persephone of Greek mythology, may bring rape and kidnap dreams. On the other hand, his reputation as a hedonistic party animal may evoke wild taboos in dreamtime. Because Pluto rules the underworld, Pluto dreams may be of the mineral kingdom: beautiful gemstones of incredible colors. Finally, Pluto dreams may be highly symbolic. The symbols may be hard to see or recognize because they involve rare subjects and intense energies or emotions. Pluto dreams may range from orgiastic to hideous. They are rarely boring or mundane!

As we have seen, the moon's relationship to the sun and the planets during a dream affects the dreaming. In addition, the moon's relationship to the dreamer's ascendant and midheaven are very important.

Ascendant Dreaming

In traditional astrological charts, the zodiacal sign that was on the horizon at the moment of birth is called the ascendant, or rising sign. One's ascendant tells an astrologer about personality. The ascendant in your soul contract represents your personal mode of behavior—style, character, and ethic. Dreams occurring when the moon is moving across your ascendant may give hints about how well you are working in the world. These dreams tend to be quite personal, usually psychological in nature, and often a little vague. However, ascendant dreams may also be perks: they may give you a little ego boost just when you need it!

Mid-heaven Dreaming

The top of your chart is called your mid-heaven. In a soul contract, your mid-heaven points directly to your soul. It represents the connection you have to the intent of your soul. When the moon crosses your mid-heaven during dreamtime, you may receive very specific messages from your higher self. The dreams may be highly symbolic and may include sounds, colors, and vibrations not ordinarily experienced in dreams. Mid-heaven dreams are often very sacred.

THE UNIVERSE IS ONE GREAT CONSCIOUSNESS

Astrology is a discipline allowing us to see the universe as one great consciousness evolving through each cell of sentience. We are part of that consciousness. We are the ecstasy of life. We are the cells of Radical Wondrousness. By studying ourselves as dreamers, we learn more about that great consciousness, and we participate more beneficently in evolution. Studying astrology in connection with dreaming helps us understand the dynamics of dreamtime.

Astrology is a massive science that includes many nuances and requires intuition as well as knowledge. Springboard off this information and learn more! As my Grannie used to say, the more you know, the more you know.

3

Thirteen Types
of Dreams

When we heal ourselves, others are healed. When we nurture our dreams, we give birth to the dreams of humankind. When we walk as loving aspects of the Earth Mother, we become fertile, life-giving Mothers of the Creative Force. When we honor our bodies, our health, and our emotional needs, we make space for our dreams to come into being. When we speak the truth from our healed hearts, we allow life abundant to continue on our Mother Planet.

JAMIE SAMS
The Thirteen Original Clan Mothers

After our circle had been meeting for just over a year, we had integrated the information about the lines of light coming from our wombs and the correlation between the moon's astrological placement and women's menstrual cycles.

To deepen our work, we decided to go on retreat, enter into dreamtime together, and stay there for several days. Debby Jameson, one of our dreaming sisters, invited us to her ranch. The setting was perfect—beautiful property in the mountains, horses to ride, a lake, and a tipi.

On our second day there, the women went to find spots of privacy and power. Each woman had set specific intent for a personal ceremony. We designed individual ceremonies to incubate our dreaming potential in order to enter the collective dream together. Everyone had gone; I settled for a nap in the tipi. I thought I was recovering from a cold—but I really had pneumonia. My priority was to heal my body.

Like pyramids, there are special energies in tipis that aren't available in ordinary sleeping places. As I drifted out of physical-self consciousness, I saw a neon white tornado spiraling toward my womb. There was no story line to this dream. In fact, there was nothing to tell except that when I awoke, I quickly grabbed my journal and wrote down an entire body of information. The information of this dream focused and restructured my work and life purpose.

I was shown that there are thirteen types of dreaming, roughly one for each of the thirteen moons in a dreamer's year. The dream types are not totally separated and distinguished, as many dreams have aspects of more than one type, nor are they definitive, as there may be other types of dreams for some people. These thirteen dream types in conjunction with the dream teachings we already practiced helped us track our patterns and become more proficient in our dream powers. The information truly moved and excited me.

At the same time, in some other corner of the Dream Weave, unbeknownst to me, Jamie Sams was creating the incredible book *The Thirteen Original Clan Mothers*. Each Clan Mother corresponds to one of the moon cycles in a lunar year. I did not know Jamie at the time, although I certainly knew of her through her Medicine Cards. A year or so later, I purchased the book and read this statement: "[Looks Far Woman, the Clan Mother of the fourth moon cycle] stands at the Crack in the Universe and safely guides human spirits taking Dream-time journeys into the other realms and then, back home, being present and fully conscious of their bodies." Looks Far Woman was with me that day in the Sierras. The "coincidence" was amazing. Subsequently, I have grown to know Jamie as an inspiring friend and an incredibly supportive sister.

PERSONAL DREAMS

The first three types of dreaming are personal. They give the dreamer specific information about her waking reality and her unfolding life process.

Mundane Dreaming

Mundane dreaming involves reworking things that were not done before you went to bed. Mundane dreams finish tasks, redo conversations that were unsatisfactory, and rearrange elements and energies of the day or the immediate past.

We rarely present mundane dreams in our dream circle because the dreamer does not have much trouble understanding them. *When a dreaming woman has a mundane dream, it means she is too tired*. Mundane dreams indicate that days are exhausting and fatigue is preventing the dreamer from entering the more subtle dreaming realms. The dreamer needs a break, a sacred retreat, or she needs to go to a spa.

Psychological Dreaming

Psychological dreaming imparts information about your personal living patterns. Mythological dreams, archetypal dreams, and dreams that give data about your own evolutionary move-ment fall into this category. Fritjof Capra, in his book *The Web of Life*, points out that new theories of living systems have created new understandings of evolution—the magnetic unfolding of life. The inherent characteristics of evolutionary systems are increasing diversity and complexity. The nature of evolution is movement toward novelty—toward a new way of being. You are constantly moving toward greater diversity and complexity in order to become new. *Psychological dreams are pointing you toward your own ultimate evolutionary destiny.*

Although we do not work much with psychological dreams in our dream circle—because the more appropriate place for that is in therapy—sometimes these dreams come up. We use psychological dreams as an opportunity to bring in informa-tion that liberates and sends the dreamer toward her destiny. While discussing psychological dreaming, we emphasize movement. We do not say that the dreamer is stuck or doing anything "wrong," and we never say "you should." This is not the arena for that.

Lucid Dreaming

Many books have been published about lucid dreaming. Most claim that it is the ultimate form of dreaming and that it is the main goal of the dreamer to achieve lucidity. Lucid dreaming occurs when the dreamer becomes aware of the dreaming in the dream. This awareness results in con-scious choices: the choice to affect the direction of the dream, and the choice to determine the degree of change. In my group, we have found that it is very helpful in a fearful or traumatic dream to become lucid and to realize that the dreamer can shift energy, or take responsibility for the dream's energy.

More importantly, we have all had experiences where we become lucid and discover that it is better not to shift the energy of the dream but instead just to be aware of the dreaming. It is often not a good idea to "take control" of dreaming. After all, we are busily "taking control" of our waking reality, and most of us have messed that up pretty well! Certainly, we can agree that collectively we are not doing so well "controlling" the world. In general, *lucid dreaming enhances the experience of the dream and blends waking and sleeping realities in an almost ideal way.* This blending occurs especially when the dreamer simply allows the dream to unfold without intervening.

Once, as I was returning to Santa Monica from New Mexico, my friend Carol was driving the car and my then-nine-year-old daughter Sara was sitting in the backseat listening to her Walkman. Just after we crossed the Arizona–California border, I nodded off. A long period of not-quite-asleep and not-quite-awake followed, and I suddenly popped into this dream:

I Died!

Connie

☽ in ♑
MOON IN CAPRICORN

I suddenly felt myself become a light being. My dream body was "riding" outside the car alongside my physical body. Carol was driving the car, Sara was singing. They didn't see me, they couldn't hear me. I was propelled by the wind outside the car. I put my dream hand through the car window into my physical body. It was dead, limp, had no feeling. Excited, I yelled, "All right! I actually died! Yes!" I got so delighted that I accidentally jumped back into my body and woke myself up.

I looked at Carol and said, "I just died." I tried to explain to her how dead it felt to be dead. There were no words to explain it—it was nothing, it was just dead. I gave up. A few hours later, when we were safely at home, the news reported a 6.3 earthquake epicentered at the exact spot where I had "died."

If I had taken control of that dream, it would have been very different. I would have been afraid. I would not have been excited and delighted by the death experience. I most certainly would not have allowed myself to fly along outside the car.

The energy of Mother Earth was particularly intense in that location in the desert. She was about to shake and crack. In some way, my physical body tuned in to that invisible reality and honored the call to shift my consciousness. An experience of life-changing proportions was my gift for honoring that call.

There is another interesting aspect of this dream: the moon was in Capricorn. In my own astrological chart, Mars is in Capricorn. When my physical body, as represented by Mars in Capricorn, and my dreaming body, as represented by the moon, aspect one another in the heavenly realm, I have lucid dreams. Look for a similar pattern in your own dreaming.

CAPRICORN DREAMING
See page 23

MARS DREAMING
See page 27

COLLECTIVE DREAMS

Collective dreams occur when your consciousness moves into the astral realm, or the realm of the collective mind. You become like a radio or television set and tune in to vibrations floating around in the collective mind. In collective dreams, you pick up on information you could not possibly know in waking reality.

Clairvoyant Dreaming

Clairvoyant dreaming involves picking up something just on the verge of manifestation. You sense something not local to you, not going on in your life, something you could not possibly know. You perceive something in the dreaming and then it tumbles into manifestation within the next twenty-four hours. Clairvoyant dreaming occurs when your consciousness expands beyond its ordinary realms. Your dream shows you something that you did not know and could not have known in ordinary consciousness. In a clairvoyant dream, you will also experience lucidity. *In other words, in a clairvoyant dream, you usually realize that you are dreaming.*

Not long ago, I dreamed I was in my office with an old boyfriend, Charles, who is a doctor. I was talking to Charles about chronic fatigue syndrome. While we were talking, the phone rang (in the dream). Sally, a dear friend, was on the line. I became lucid in my dream and moved through the phone lines into Sally's living room. Marvin, her husband, was running around the room being very petulant and throwing his socks. We made fun of him and laughed. That was my dream.

Early the next morning, Sally called. I thought she and Marvin were still out of the country, so I was surprised and delighted to hear from her. She told me that Marvin had been an absolute child for the past couple of days, and she was laughing at him. I could hear him ranting about something in the background. About noon that day, Charles called. He said he had been thinking of calling for several days. I hadn't spoken with him in over three years. I was astonished but had the presence of mind to ask about chronic fatigue syndrome. He actually had a lot to say about the disease and sent me some very helpful information.

I do not know how it happens, but in clairvoyant dreaming you simply pick up on thoughts, plans, and possibilities that hover around.

Telepathic Dreaming

Telepathic dreaming is also nonlocal; that is, you receive information unavailable in waking reality. The telepathic dream, however, is about something that has already occurred, something that already exists in manifestation.

Telepathic dreams are very realistic. In telepathic dreams, you are so sure you are not dreaming that you cannot possibly awaken in the dream—it's the opposite of lucidity. Telepathic dreams are realistic because the dreamer picks up on a vibration that already exists in manifestation; the vibration is already in form.

Peggy had been attending dream circle for several years. Through her work in dreamtime, her life path had clarified itself. She realized she needed to return to graduate school to acquire the proper qualifications for her life work. However, financial aid was necessary to make this plan possible. Applying for school admission and waiting for financial-aid approval were stressful.

Peggy

☽ void into ♎

☿

MOON VOID
MOVING INTO LIBRA
ASPECTING MERCURY

MERCURY DREAMING
See page 26

Acceptance

A man bursts into the room with papers spilling out of his arms. I know, somehow, that he is the admissions officer at the university. He tells me that I have been accepted but will have to wait a little longer to hear about my financial aid.

The next day Peggy received an acceptance letter in the mail. Notice that the moon aspected Mercury that night— a perfect night to receive telepathic information. The stress remained because she knew that without financial aid she could not attend school. Peggy felt that if she were accepted but unable to attend, the disappointment would be hard.

Twelve Units

I was reading a piece of paper that said I had received enough money from financial-aid sources to take twelve units [full time].

Peggy

☽ void into ♎
☿

MOON VOID
MOVING INTO LIBRA
ASPECTING MERCURY

The morning after Peggy had this dream, she knew that the letter would be in her mailbox when she got home, and it was. Both of Peggy's dreams are telepathic, because the letters were already in the mail when she had the dreams.

Also, please notice that the moon was in the same astrological position when Peggy dreamed the two dreams. Her natal moon is in the sign of Libra. These two dreams indicate that Peggy has a particular bias toward telepathic dreaming when the moon goes void, of course, just before it moves into Libra as well as when the moon aspects Mercury.

LIBRA DREAMING
See page 22

Prophetic Dreaming

Prophetic, or precognitive, dreams foresee the future. The information in a prophetic dream is not previously known; that is, the information is not in the known data field. Prophecy resides in the realm of possibility rather than probability. Clairvoyant dreams have to do with probability; probability is a denser vibration than possibility because it is already moving toward manifestation. Telepathy deals with what already exists in form, so telepathic dreams are quite solid in nature.

Because prophecy resides in a less dense frequency, prophetic dreams are usually symbolic and hard to recognize. The feedback from clairvoyant or telepathic dreams is immediate—within a few days. The feedback from prophetic dreams may occur so far into the future that either you forget you have had the dream or you never make the connection.

For example, I had a series of dreams in which something bizarre was growing out of my legs. One time, I dreamed of a very dark moon-shaped tumorlike growth on my right leg. Another time, there was prairie grass on my knee. Another time, fish heads grew out of my leg pores. In every dream, I had a skin-crawling sensation when I looked at my legs—and even now, as I type these words, I have that sense of *yuck*. In my dreams, I was afraid to remove the growths because they were very deeply rooted in the leg—perhaps bone-deep.

In dream circle, all sorts of theories floated around about these dreams, but none really fit. Then one day I heard someone make a comment about legs: legs are the human's sacred earth connection. When I heard that statement, an oracular voice said "earthquake." I ran to my journals and looked up all these dreams. Sure enough, in each case, eighteen to twenty-one days after the dream we had a 6.3 or higher earthquake in Southern California. I had not made that connection, nor had I ever really understood the symbols.

I researched the quakes. The dream with the fish growing out of my legs prophesied a quake epicentered in the ocean between Santa Monica and Catalina Island. The quake prophesied by prairie grass was epicentered in the hills above Malibu. The dream with the dark moon-shaped tumor prophesied the big quake of January 1994 that came at night on a dark moon. *Prophetic dreams usually have a phenomenal aspect to them.* After you've read the definition of phenomenal dreaming later in this chapter, think about your own prophetic patterns.

PHENOMENAL
DREAMING
See page 49

Prophetic dreaming is quite useful, as you can imagine. Since I realized the nature of my prophetic dreams, I have been very accurate with prophecy work. Realizing the gift increases the gift's power.

DREAMING
THE GREATER
CONSCIOUSNESS

Beyond the human collective consciousness, there is a greater awareness that presents itself in certain dreaming circumstances. The dreams that move beyond the human collective involve learning or doing something in dreaming that changes ordinary reality. These dreams are usually altruistic in nature and call the dreamer to assist others. They come from the higher self, or the soul self, which sees the interconnectedness of all universes and dimensions.

Teaching Dreaming

In teaching dreams, you learn a new aspect of your earth walk. Your soul speaks to you about what you are here to be and what you are here to become. However, teaching dreams are different in character and texture from psychological dreams. They change your deepest understanding of yourself and your powers to heal. Creative dreams, dreams that inspire you to be artistic, belong to this category. "Medicine" dreams, dreams where you learn something about your unique alignment with Great Creator, are also teaching dreams.

The teacher in teaching dreams may be your higher self, or it may actually be an ascended master who has come to speak to you. Llewellyn Vaughan-Lee in his book *In the Company of Friends: Dreamwork within a Sufi Cult* documents many occasions when a dead guru or master appeared in the dreams of students to further their practice. However, often an image of a living teacher will appear. The following is an example of a teaching dream.

Turn Around

I was stuck in a chamber in a pyramid. I could not figure out how to get out, nor could I remember how I got in. I was beginning to panic when I noticed movement in the west corner. I had thought it was a sculpture, but now I could see that it was Connie. She came over to me and said, "Turn around and see that you are dreaming. It's the only way out." I could not understand what she was saying—I understood the words, but I could not figure out how to do it.

As James wrote down the dream the next morning, he realized he had received an important teaching. "Turn around and look at yourself dreaming" is the ultimate dream teaching, is it not? Look at every action and meditation—every waking or sleeping vision—as the dream.

This is a very important aspect of teaching dreams: *the teacher is usually you.* When my clients report dreams in which I have apparently brought them a dream teaching, I always remind them that the message was so important that they really needed to remember it. To help ensure memory, they assigned a familiar teacher's face to the messenger. Of course, there may be times when you are "visited" in a dream. But usually your higher self is your own master teacher. James saw me at the foot of his bed, but most likely that was his own higher self wearing my face so that he would pay attention to the message.

Teaching dreams have proved to be highly catalytic for dreamers. They contain information that does not actually originate in the dreamer's being; therefore, they indicate that the dreamer has been on a different plane of consciousness. Teaching dreams literally change the vibration of the work that the dreamer does in waking reality. Fritjof Capra tells us in *The Web of Life* that many famous physicists, specifically John von

Neumann and Norbert Wiener, had the habit of sleeping with pencil and paper near their beds because teaching dreams were common experiences for them. We might all do well to follow their example.

Healing Dreaming

The dreamer helps someone move toward wholeness in healing dreams.

Madeleine, a doctor and holistic healer, had been working energetically with her mother for two years to heal a lung cancer. When the cancer first appeared, they began a program of herbs, vitamins, and energetic healing. This cancer involved a blood vessel—a sure sign of future recurrent disease according to Western medicine. After a relatively short period of working with alternative cures, Madeleine's mother went for surgery. The cancer was "gone." It had necrosed, or died. However, the doctors were confident that it would reappear within six months.

Madeleine and her mother continued holistic therapy. Two years later, x-rays came back that read "highly diagnostic of," "consistent with," and "cannot rule out" bone cancer. The cancer had spread from the lung to the bone in the right shoulder. Madeleine immediately went to her mother's home and had this dream:

Relieve the Pain

Madeleine

☽ in ♋
MOON IN CANCER

Mother is sitting in a chair in front of me. I am waving my hands over her. "Now what's that supposed to do?" she asks. "Relieve the pain," I answer. "Oh. Oh yeah. I can feel that," she responds matter-of-factly. Then I was just holding my hands over her and allowing the energy to flow through me. "How about that?" she says. "Feels good, warm."

The next day Madeleine watched with gratitude as her mother hung a Santa Claus kite on a hook from the rafters outside the house. She was standing on her tiptoes extending her right arm completely above her head, a range of movement that was impossible the day before. About a week later, the radiologist repeated the scans and discovered that Madeleine's mother did not have cancer. Note the irony that this dream came when the moon was in the sign of Cancer. Dreamtime is often pun time!

In Madeleine's case, the dreamer healed the patient. In other cases, a healer comes to heal the dreamer. If this happens, it is usually because by being healed, you will either learn a technique or carry a new energy that will help others. *Healing dreams are always altruistic in nature.*

Healing dreams, like teaching dreams, change the reality of the dreamer and the patient. If you dream that you heal someone and this someone literally wakes up feeling better the next day, it is very hard to doubt yourself as a powerful dreamer. Similarly, if you dream that you are "doctored" and wake up feeling better, with an instruction about how to pass that healing on, you are changed. Healing dreams transform you!

Oracular Dreaming

Oracle is a Greek word referring to revealing hidden information. The oracle is a divine utterance. Oracular information brings guidance to the dreamer. *Oracular dreaming is wisdom from the divine realm transferred directly—not through visual symbols but through words.* The oracle often comes in a riddle or in ambiguous terminology. Oracles are puzzles. In oracular dreams, you might be given a name or a chant. Oracular dreams are times when Great Dreamer is speaking directly to you as a dreaming woman, and it is up to you and your circle to learn and understand the dream.

DREAMS OF DANCING THE WEAVE

Dreams of dancing the weave require moving one's consciousness into a more expanded arena. These dreams sometimes involve "dreaming together": you bump into friends or dreaming partners on the weave and "dance" together. The dreams result in a change of waking reality, although the change is not always as trackable as that of healing, teaching, or oracular dreaming.

Ceremonial Dreaming

When ceremonial dreams occur, the dreamer appears at a ceremony in the dream realm and works with other dreamers to manifest something. This something may or may not be recognizable, and the other dreamers may or may not be known to you. Ceremonial dreaming is a higher octave of teaching dreaming. In ceremonial dreaming, you are "intending the world"; that is, you are using intent.

Intent, in its purest form, does not originate in the individual's personal will. Intent is a force that exists within the Weave with which the dreamer may align. "Intending the world" means aligning yourself with potential, the Great Dreamer, or God, if you will. Alignment with intent reveals your "medicine," because it shows you how to call power and use it for beneficial purposes.

When you align with intent for dreaming, you allow energy to move through you in order to manifest itself in form. Ceremonial dreaming involves joining other dreamers to align with intent. The dream is more powerful when many dreamers work together, just as a collective ceremony is more powerful than an individual ceremony. You may have dreams that involve ceremony which do not include other dreamers. These are usually teaching dreams. *Ceremonial dreams involve other dreamers all aligning with intent.*

Beating the Earth Drum

Jeanne

☽ in ♈

MOON IN ARIES

It is a very dark night with lots of stars. I enter an area which is a dirt mound like an amphitheater. Connie and the dreaming women are all facing one direction sitting on the mound. We are there to contact another tribe not yet identified. We know the tribe is there. We are each given two bundles of long thin wooden twigs. They are made of dark red/brown wood. I take my place and sit cross-legged on the ground and hit the bundles of twigs onto the earth like beaters on a drum. We are all doing this in rhythm together. This signals the other tribe. A message in smoke letters is sent into the air from our drumming. It lingers there about twelve feet above the ground. I think it was a name identifying us. Our beating sends up other lights around and above us.

When it is over, we leave the mound and enter the theater section. The floors are wooden. I hear Connie say to a dreaming sister, "We lost three or four." I'm concerned. I know the outcome was not known to us while we were doing it, but I hadn't perceived danger or loss of sisters. I wanted to tell Connie this, and so I went up to her while she was talking. I waited. Then I realized she meant three or four dreaming sisters left during the ceremony. "Lost" didn't mean "died," it meant they left the work.

The dreamers in Jeanne's dream came together in ceremony to evoke helpful energies from other realms. We may never know exactly what the ceremony accomplished, but its holy nature and sense of sacred gathering certainly indicate that the ceremony was "real." The dreamer often awakens from a ceremonial dream with only a lingering sense of divine presence as validation for the reality of the event.

Shamanic Dreaming

The shaman lives, literally and metaphorically, at the edge of the village—at the edge of consciousness, if you will. The shaman is not quite a part of the social structure and not quite a part of the jungle. The shaman is a bridge between the universes, in the world but not of it. Shamanic dreaming involves journeying into other worlds in search of information for someone else's healing. Shamanic dreams are shape-shifting dreams, underworld dreams, dreams in which the dreamer's frame of reference changes profoundly.

In shamanic dreams, the dreamer communicates with dead people, ancestors, fairies, animals, or angels. The dreams involve direct communication with realms that are virtually inaccessible. The information from them is for the purpose of healing the planet, the circle, or the client. If the dreamer needs healing, a different type of energy is evoked.

Shamanic dreaming is rare. It demands special circumstances, and it requires a very sophisticated sensitivity. I've heard shamanic dreams from my teachers. I've had only one myself. These dreams are too personal, too private, too fragile to use as examples. You know when you've had one. You know what to do with it.

Phenomenal Dreaming

Phenomenal dreaming breaks the laws of the physical world in some kind of synchronistic way. Of course, we break the laws of the world all the time in dreaming, but not many dreams constitute phenomenal dreaming. *A dream is phenomenal when there is a synchronistic and serendipitous waking reality correspondent to it.*

In phenomenal dreams, the dreamer goes into parallel universes with somebody else. Then something in waking reality mirrors that experience. Usually it becomes very clear to the dreamer through feedback that they have dreamed someone else's dream. The synchronistic element, the waking-world feedback, is the key.

Phenomenal dreams include a change of energies and/or circumstances that are echoed in waking reality. They are different from telepathic or clairvoyant dreams because the dreamer actually causes the change. Phenomenal dreams are not prophetic, because they are in present time, and they are synchronistic. In phenomenal dreams, the veils between waking and sleeping disappear.

Madeleine taught at the University of California at Los Angeles (UCLA) Medical School for many years. Eventually, she left UCLA to pursue a practice that incorporated a wider variety of healing techniques. Shortly after that, she moved out of her home for several months to have reconstruction work done. Madeleine did not notify anyone at UCLA where to find her because she thought her work there was terminated. She had been out of her house for several months when she had this dream:

There She Is, Get Her

Madeleine

☽ in ♋

MOON IN CANCER

I had an office at UCLA. It was beautiful with very comfortable leather furniture. However, I could not get in it because the nurses were always using it for their meetings.

I came out of my office and entered an auditorium. There were two men in black leather outfits and helmets that looked over at me and said, "There she is, get her!" One guy came after me, and I used several moves and karate punches to knock him out. It was almost too easy, like punching a marshmallow. His helmet fell back, revealing his face. He was pale, very light blue eyes and dishwater blond hair.

I tried to use several phones to call someone to report the incident. All of the phone lines had been cut. Finally I used the emergency phone like the ones UCLA has on campus. They asked me if it were an emergency. I said, "Why, yes." They said they would send someone.

I saw my nurse Susie, who is a Chinese woman, and asked her to come over and bear witness to what had occurred.

Shortly after this dream, Madeleine returned to UCLA to perform a procedure on a patient. Madeleine's privileges were delayed three weeks because of some nursing regulations (*meetings of nurses in her office*). When she went back to work, Madeleine was greeted with open arms, and she felt really comfortable being back there (*comfortable office*).

On her second day at work, Madeleine was called out of her office to the front desk because she had a visitor. She was not expecting anyone and felt anticipatory as she walked down the hall to the open area (*auditorium*). To her surprise, a man in black leather pants and a black helmet handed her a piece of paper, a summons for a wrongful-death lawsuit (*get her!*). Madeleine had consulted on a case previously and had seen a certain patient twice. The patient had died some years ago and the family was now suing the UCLA doctors.

When Madeleine contacted the attorney who was handling the case, he told her he had been trying to reach her for months, but because of her home restoration, the phone had been disconnected (*cut phone lines*).

When Madeleine showed up for the deposition, she was astonished to see that the face of the man suing her was the face of the man she had knocked out in her dream. Furthermore, the court reporter, Sandy, was a Chinese woman (*Susie, the witness in the dream*).

All these elements are incredible, but the dream could still be seen as telepathic since the lawsuit was real—it had already manifested when Madeleine had the dream. Read on. This next part is the *phenomenal* part.

Despite continued warnings from her attorney not to volunteer too much information, Madeleine spoke truthfully and freely in the deposition. The prosecuting attorney (who was also the plaintiff) asked many direct questions. Madeleine gave direct answers (*karate moves*). By the end of the day, the tough attorney had softened into the grieving son of a beloved father. He thanked Madeleine for taking care of his dad in his last days, and he dropped the lawsuit (*like punching a marshmallow*).

Madeleine's dream prepared her energetic body for the upcoming lawsuit—one that could have been devastating to her life and career. Because of the dream, Madeleine had her tools ready. She caused a change in the dream that mirrored itself in waking reality. At the time of the dream, Madeleine had no idea that she would soon be returning to UCLA, nor did she know anything about the legal action. Her dreaming, however, prepared her for both.

Madeleine's dream represents phenomenal dreaming. When the events were presented, Madeleine knew how to respond. She knew the marshmallow nature of the plaintiff, and she knew she was in a place of power and could transform the experience for him. Madeleine not only changed the possibilities for herself, the other doctors, and UCLA, but she also transformed the hurting man. Madeleine took the man down the path of dreaming and gave him healing from his own pain.

Sacred Dreaming

Sacred dreams occur under unusual circumstances—for example, a life-threatening illness or the death of a loved one. These dreams often have no story line, but they involve vivid colors, sounds, geometric shapes, and/or intense sensations. The dreamer awakens from sacred dreams with a stronger sense of her life purpose. Sometimes there is exact information conveyed in the dream, and sometimes there is just a knowingness. The dreamer has peeked at her soul contract!

The neon-tornado dream at the beginning of this chapter could certainly be defined as a sacred dream. The pneumonia in my lungs created an interesting state of consciousness. In one sense, I was in full-time meditation, because each and every breath was my main point of focus. I was primarily aware of the need to breathe slowly and evenly in order to prevent a coughing spasm. The slow, easy breaths evoked the neon tornado, and the tornado moved directly into my womb, my knowing space, my dreaming vessel. I awoke with the teaching of the thirteen types of dreaming.

NEON-TORNADO DREAM
See page 34

I have read that Einstein "dreamed" the theory of relativity, not as a story line but as a geometric picture. Legend has it that he awoke, scribbled down the now famous equation ($E=mc^2$), and went back to sleep. When he awoke the next morning, his life and the lives of us all were changed forever. If true, Einstein's dream must have been the ultimate sacred dream.

Sacred dreams do not come often, and they do not come to everyone. Instead, perhaps I could say that not everyone remembers sacred dreams. One must have the vocabulary to transform the vibration of sacred dreaming into words. And certainly not everyone has devoted a lifetime to developing sacred-dream vocabulary.

LOOKS FAR WOMAN
See page 35

Looks Far Woman teaches us that every human being has the ability to use information found in dreams to change the course of life. Looks Far Woman sees all potential truths, shows us how to observe everything around us, and shows us how to remember every detail.

I give thanks that Looks Far Woman walks with me. I hope that the teachings she showed me through my sacred dream help you develop the sacred dreamer in yourself.

4

Charting the Dream

It is true that dreams without action, without "product," have given the dreamer a bad name. It is also more than true that action without vision has given our species a bad name. . . . Dreamers who produce are the most valuable citizens in the world. They are the true leaders of society.

THOMAS LANE
The Artists' Manifesto

Great Dreamer is dreaming a change of consciousness at this time in our evolution. She is giving us all the assistance and information we need in our dreaming. However, we must receive it, perceive it, and put it to work. We are birthing ourselves into a new species. Dreaming is our midwife.

When a woman gives birth, especially for the first time, she learns the meaning of trust. The mother has studied, practiced, and learned. Then the moment is at hand, and it is bigger than expected. The mental preparation helped, but in fact, the physical experience is all there is! The mother knows only that her body is moving toward something she cannot control, something she wants very much, and something she prays to the very core of her being will be good.

The midwife or doctor doesn't know what the baby will look like or how well it will function, but they do know all the birth patterns intimately, and they work in joy and faith. The midwife's wisdom, experience, and peace of mind are contagious. Everyone involved in the birthing trusts the process.

After birth, nature provides everyone with the energy and knowingness to do what is required next.

Dreaming and giving birth have two aspects in common that I will discuss in this chapter: doing the homework and surrendering to the process.

DOING THE HOMEWORK

This section reads like a how-to manual. But it is necessary. Homework is homework! Just read carefully and follow the logic of the work, and you will see that the work is easy and well worth the effort. However, do not get bogged down in the charting process. Like the previous chapters, this chapter is a guideline. Read it. Practice it. But don't let the work stop you from moving.

A woman's natural cycles determine her dreaming. Her physical and emotional cycles connect directly to the moon. How she honors her cycles, what she knows about them, and how her awarenesses attune to them are all factors in her relationship to dreaming. When a woman follows the cycles of her nature, the cycles of Mother Nature, she knows herself to be sourced in truth and spiritual abundance.

The most important natural cycle for a woman is the lunar cycle. As previously mentioned, the moon and a woman's dreaming are inseparable. Every woman has thirteen cycles in her dreaming year. This may or may not parallel a twelve-month year on the sun calendar. The year I mean is a "year" measured in cycles of thirteen lunar months. The first day of a woman's dreaming cycle is the first day of her bleeding. In other words, every time a woman is on her moon and begins to bleed, she starts a new dreaming cycle. Then she numbers the days consecutively until the next bleeding begins. Thirteen of those cycles represent a dreamer's year.

If one does not bleed, is post-menopausal, has had a hysterectomy, is pre-menses, or is a man, the dreaming cycle starts on the day of the month the moon returns to the *exact* position it held on the day of birth. You can read this off your astrological chart. That day is a moon power day. In other words, I was born with the moon at 28 degrees and 40 minutes of Gemini. Every month when the moon moves through Gemini and hits 28°40′, that is a moon power day for me. My moon power day will be the first day of my dreaming cycle when I am post-menopausal.

It is important to know when one's dreaming cycles begin and end, because that is the first homework step of dreaming. If you do not have an astrological chart, your first homework assignment is to get one. Call a reputable astrologer or find an astrology service. You don't need a reading—just a chart.

THE DREAM JOURNAL

Keep a dream journal. Every day include the following information: the date, the astrological location of the moon, the phase of the moon, any other lunar information, the day of your cycle, the title of the dream, the content of the dream, and some information about what is going on in waking reality.

At the end of each cycle, all these bits of information are recorded on a pie chart to give you a picture of your dreaming.

The date: I usually record my dreams in the morning just after I get up. I put the date as the morning date, even though I know I may have had the dream before midnight. That way I will know I am writing on the 31st of January what I dreamed on the night of the 30th. Example: 1-31-99.

The astrological location of the moon: Refer to your *Pocket Astrologer* calendar to learn the moon's location during the dream. Sometimes the moon goes void of course during dreaming, or moves between two signs. That is always worth noting. Example: 1-31-99, Leo.

The phase of the moon: You can also discern the moon's phase from the astrological calendar. The moon's phase becomes important later as you track your own dreaming cycles. Example: 1-31-99, Leo, Full Moon.

Other astrological information: Some days might have additional aspects that are important to note. An eclipse, a personal moon power day, or the moon aspecting another planet may all occur on a dreaming night. Example: 1-31-99, Leo, Full Moon, Lunar Eclipse, Blue Moon.

The day of your cycle: If you are a woman who still has menstrual cycles, make note of where you are in your cycle when you write down a dream. Day one of a cycle is the first day you start bleeding. Then number the days consecutively until the next month when you start bleeding again. At the end of each cycle, look back over your month of dreaming and cross-reference the dreams on a pie chart similar to the example provided. If for any reason you no longer have bleeding cycles or you are a man, chart your cycles according to your moon power day. Example: 1-31-99, Leo, Full Moon, Lunar Eclipse, Blue Moon, Day 22.

PIE CHART
See page 63

Dream title: A dream title is a mental shortcut. A title gives word cues to remind you of the dream. It's strictly for use on the charting process explained below.

The dream: Now write the dream(s). Every dreamer may choose how she does this, but the point is to record the dream story and include as many details as possible.

The type of dream: If you can see immediately that your dream fits into one of the thirteen types, make a note. Often the dream type is hard to know until you share it with your dream circle or see the dream event manifest. Do not worry too much about this particular category if your dream type is not perfectly obvious.

Waking reality: It is also important to include something about each day's waking reality. This is because we are in a dreaming process that involves the waking world. It does not really matter if you include something about your own life, something mundane, something from the news, or something political. Just trust yourself. Write what comes to mind. It will be exactly what you are going to need later.

Here is an example from one of my dreaming journals:

Oklahoma *Reunion*

I was on a train. I didn't know where I was going. Somehow I knew when to get off. It was an old Western town, like the train station in Oklahoma. We were having a big family reunion.

It was time to change clothes. I went to my closet. I discovered new things behind the old. They were exactly appropriate—one red sweater I really liked.

Waking: Dream circle with Heather. I shared the dream about the wild dog and yellow feces. She was masterful.

Connie
1-31-99
☽ in ♌
MOON IN LEO
FULL MOON
LUNAR ECLIPSE
BLUE MOON
DAY 22

Now in one journal entry I have all the information I need to help chart my dreaming.

THE PIE CHART

At the end of each cycle, transfer the information to a circle graph or pie chart. The graph consists of a large circle with a smaller concentric circle inside. These two circles are divided into four quadrants.

Around the outside of the chart, put the number of your cycle days. Place day one at the top of the circle, and then put all the other days in relatively equal spaces around the chart in clockwise direction. I usually put seven days in the first quadrant, which includes the days I'm bleeding and perhaps one or two days after. In the second quadrant, I put the seven or eight days before my ovulation. In the third quadrant, I put the week after ovulation. In the last quadrant, I put the seven to nine days before I start bleeding. In other words, the quadrants may not necessarily represent the exact same number of days, because you may not have a twenty-eight-day cycle every month. I range from twenty-six to thirty-five days. When I'm charting my dreams, I make the adjustments on the chart. If you don't know exactly when you ovulate, just divide the dreams from the middle of your cycle into the second and third quadrants.

It is also important to put the calendar date next to the day of your cycle. These charts are references. They do not contain all the information of the dreams. At some point later you may want to look up the journal entry of a dream on the chart, and having the date will be vital.

The space between the larger and smaller circles is for astrological information. In other words, in the band created

PIE CHART
See page 63

COMPUTER CHART
See page 67

by the two circles next to Day 1 (12-29), outside the big circle, write the symbol for Scorpio (or wherever the moon was that night). Finally, put the dream titles for each night inside the second circle. Outside the circles, next to the cycle day and date, write the waking-reality information from your journal. I have provided two examples on the following pages: a blank form and a completed form.

After you have compiled these circle graphs for several months, you will begin to see patterns. You will have certain types of dreams in certain astrological signs. This relates to the fact that as the moon goes through specific signs of the zodiac, she plucks your light lines like a harp string. The vibration sent through your system determines the dreaming images you experience at that time.

The pie chart is primarily to help you study your personal patterns as they relate to your menstrual, or moon power, cycle. I have included an explanation of the pie chart in this chapter because it is highly important to you as an individual dreamer. However, in other chapters of this book I have not always included the dreamer's cycle day when reporting dreams. Personal cycles are unique to each dreamer, and in later chapters, I will be referring to the collective nature of dreams. But before you can fully understand the collective nature of dreams, you must understand your personal patterns.

STUDY YOUR PATTERNS

Every woman's dreaming pattern is different. A woman's pattern depends on her own cycles and her own relationship to the energies of the zodiac. This is why you must do your homework. You must know your own cycles before you can fully understand collective dreaming.

Dream Chart

Name: _____

Beginning Date: _____

Closing Date: _____

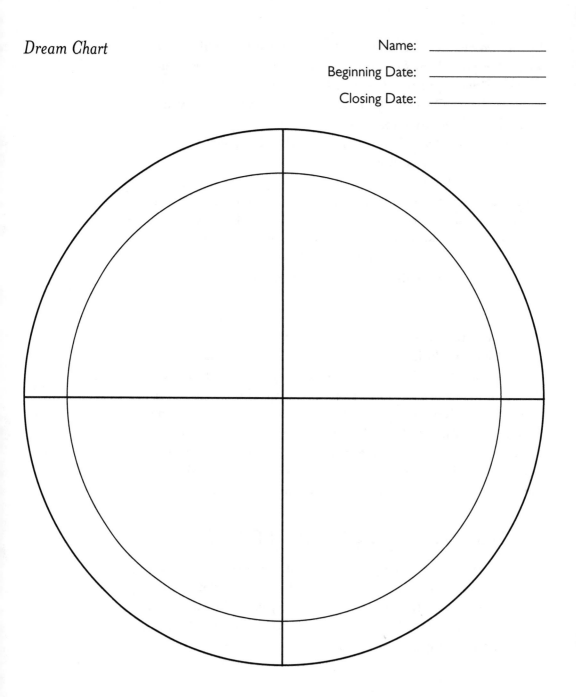

Dream Chart

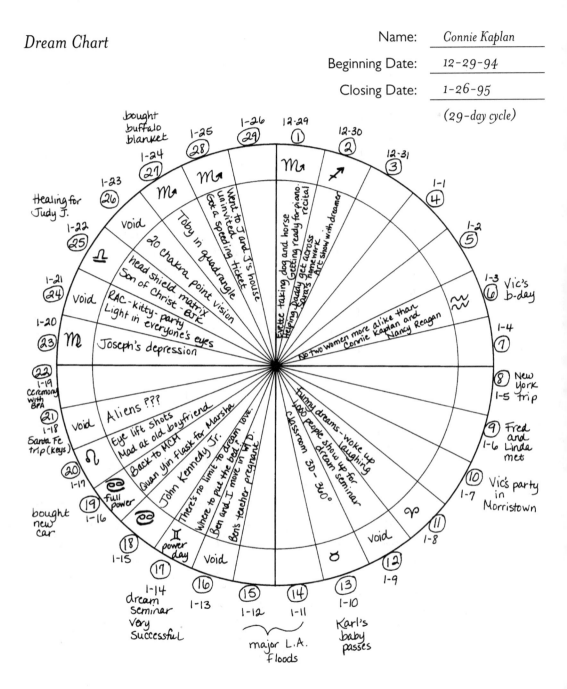

bought buffalo blanket
1-25 ㉘
1-26 ㉙
12-29 ①
12-30 ②
12-31 ③
1-24 ㉗
1-23 ㉖ Healing for Judy J.
1-1 ④
1-22 ㉕ void
1-2 ⑤
Toby in quadrangle
Went to J and J's house uninvited. Got a speeding ticket
20 chakra point vision
head shield matrix
Son of Christ - BK
RAC - kitty - party
Light in everyone's eyes
Evette taking dog and horse
Helping Sarah get across Daddy getting ready for piano recital
Art show with dreamer
No two women more alike than Connie Kaplan and Nancy Reagan
1-3 ⑥ Vic's b-day
1-21 ㉔ void
1-4 ⑦
1-20 ㉓ Joseph's depression
1-5 ⑧ New York trip
1-19 ㉒ ceremony with BrA
1-6 ⑨ Fred and Linda met
1-18 ㉑ Santa Fe trip (keys)
void
Aliens ???
Eye lift shots
Mad at old boyfriend
Back to MCH
Quan Yin flask for Marsha
John Kennedy Jr.
There's no limit to dream love.
Where to put the bed; Ben and I move in w/ D.
Ben's teacher - pregnant.
Funny dreams - woke up laughing
1,000 people show up for classroom dream seminar
3D - 360°
1-7 ⑩ Vic's party in Morristown
1-17 ⑳
1-16 ⑲ full power
bought new car
1-15 ⑱
power day
1-8 ⑪ void
1-9 ⑫
1-10 ⑬ Karl's baby passes
1-14 ⑰ dream seminar very successful
1-13 ⑯
1-12 ⑮
1-11 ⑭
major L.A. floods

63

Let me share some things I learned about myself after only six months of charting my dreaming in this way:

Every month, when the moon is in Libra, my main dream character is my sister, who is a double Libra.

Many of my upsetting dreams come when the moon is in my rising sign, Aquarius. These are usually dreams telling me I am holding on to some psychological habit no longer of service to me.

All my oracular dreams—dreams containing dreaming information or instruction about dream circle—come when the moon is void of course. I was born when the moon was void of course, and both my children were born when the moon was void of course. That is unusual. Usually when the moon is between signs, everything stops.

My heaviest dreaming comes on days 6–10 and 16–21 of my cycle. I rarely remember dreams on days 3 and 4 (my heaviest bleeding days).

TIME EFFICIENCY

One valuable result of charting dreams is time efficiency. For example, if one were to learn through charting that she tends to have prophetic dreams during a Capricorn moon and psychological dreams during an Aquarius moon, she would be able to understand this dreaming more efficiently. If she dreams of an earthquake when the moon is in Aquarius, she knows she is in for an internal shake-up (psychological dream). If, however, she dreams of an earthquake when the moon is in Capricorn, she should check her first-aid kits and supplies of extra food and water. That is time efficiency!

Charting also helps you trust dreaming. We are in the habit of believing that dreams are personal, disconnected from humanity, and nonrelated to the cycles of nature. However, the combination of discovering your own repeating dreaming cycles and learning that other people dream similar images to yours teaches you that dreaming is connected, collective, and an expansion of your ordinary reality. You start to trust your gift.

OTHER WAYS TO CHART

After charting your dreams in the pie chart for a while, you may also find other useful types of cross-referencing. In addition to a monthly chart, some women keep a yearly cycle chart simply listing the dream titles astrologically in a notebook.

You can keep this type of a yearly chart by making a notebook with a page representing each astrological sign. Then list the titles of all the dreams you have had when the moon was in the sign designated on each page. A pattern of what kinds of dreams you have in Libra, for example, will begin to emerge. You will also see that you dream seasonally: winter dreams are different from spring, summer, and fall dreams. But you will see that one year's winter dreams are surprisingly similar to another year's winter dreams.

Some women have noticed uncanny similarities between dreams on certain days of the year. For example, I have very similar—and very spiritual—dreams on April Fools Day every year.

Another valuable cross-reference is to make note of recurring dream symbols on index cards. Note on the cards when and under what conditions you dream those symbols. You will see that you tend to dream specific symbols at specific times of the month. I have noticed that anger dreams occur on the fifteenth, sixteenth, and seventeenth days of my cycle. I am not an "angry woman," and it used to disturb me when that kind of intensity erupted in dreaming. A therapist might leap at those dreams and look for repressed childhood feelings. As it turns out, I have anger dreams when I ovulate. My dreaming organs are passionately exploding! It is that simple and that beautiful. It is also very helpful to know when one ovulates, don't you think?

COMPUTERIZED CHARTING

Of course, if you are computer literate, you may find it extremely efficient to set up a database chart. Each time I fill a dream journal (about every six months), I go back through and computerize my dreams. I created a simple database with a field for each important piece of information: day, month, year, moon position, moon phase, my cycle phase, other moon aspects, and a brief dream description. I also created three or four columns for major symbols. Sometimes I want to look at all the dreams I have had when I was ovulating. I go to the database and match all dreams on the fourteenth or fifteenth day of my cycle. Boom, I can see the patterns quickly. Computerized charting is fascinating.

That, in a nutshell, is your homework. Believe it or not, it does not require mastery of astrology, although everything you know about the energies of the zodiac helps. Mostly, your homework requires sensitivity to energies as well as minimal note taking and organizing. Many dreamers find themselves resisting charts. Be gentle with yourself if you do. Keep the journal. Chart as often as you can. But don't judge or stress yourself. When the time is right, something will motivate you to know your patterns, and you'll do the work! It's profoundly rewarding and self-supportive when you finally begin to see yourself and your patterns!

Dream Symbols Chart—Red
Connie Kaplan

DATE	MOON	DAY	DREAM DESCRIPTION	NOTES
11-6-92	♈	19	Red carpet—magic carpet ride	
12-27-92	♒ ♃	12	Larry's hair on fire—bright red	
11-26-93	♉ ♃	12	Nancy spills red wine into center of earth. Birthday party—red robe, red dress, red sequined cowboy hat	
2-24-94	♌ ♃	16	CC and Carol crash my red Saab	
4-11-94	void ☿ ♃	26	New dream teachings— blood on tissue	Teaching dream
7-28-94	♈	22	Anais Nin party— Freya dresses me in red	
9-16-94	♒ ♃	10	Man in red polyester	
10-11-94	♑ ♃	9	Ben's soccer coach—red hair	Barbara didn't recognize me at restaurant
10-29-94	void	27	Strange red blood creatures on upper leg	
11-23-94	void ♃	22	Birth of sacred child—can't find pads—much blood	
12-5-94	♑	6	Daddy's red Bible	
3-16-95	♍ ♄ ♃	10	Red limo to Ceta Canyon	

On the preceding page, I have provided an example of my computerized dream symbols chart. I told my computer to pull up all the dreams with the symbol *red* in them. Please notice that many of my "red" dreams came when the moon was aspecting Jupiter. Any ideas why? Just coincidence? I think not.

POWER-DAY DREAMS

Every woman has at least two moon power days every month. Each month the moon goes through every sign of the zodiac. When the moon duplicates the sign and degree it was in on your birth date, you have a moon power day. Also, the moon moves through all phases—full, quarter, new, etc.—each month. When the moon duplicates the exact phase it was in on your birthday, that is also a moon power day. You have your most important dreams of the month on your moon power days. It is important to pay special attention to them.

One day each year, within two weeks of your birthday, the moon will duplicate the exact sign, degree, and phase of your birth. That is a dreamer's most powerful day of the year. That's the day when you dream a dream of your next cycle's intent. On your *big* power day, Great Dreamer gives a preview of your coming year!

My moon was at 28 degrees and 40 minutes of Gemini when I was born. The moon was full and void of course. Every month when the moon returns to 28°40′ Gemini, I have a power day. Every full moon is a power day. I also have a powerful dreaming experience every time the moon goes void of course. Once a year, I have a *big* power day. True dreamers ceremonialize that day. In fact, a tradition in my circles is to party on the dreamer's birthday and create ceremony on the big moon power day!

It is exciting and important to know these things about yourself. Every shred of information about your dreaming gives more value to the whole process of your life.

The Maya were extraordinarily skilled at measuring cycles accurately. They created a calendar based on the thirteen lunar cycles. They had knowledge and wisdom that expressed time as a dimension rather than a linear movement. Charting your dreaming cycles on thirteen pie charts does much more than give you an organization of your dreams—it honors what your body knows to be an accurate measurement of your cycles. Charting on thirteen pie charts aligns you with galactic timing because it reawakens the memory of living in a cyclical system that, like the universe, is ever expanding. This type of charting expands your consciousness.

Remember, women access knowledge directly through their wombs. Everything you need to know you already know, but putting your knowledge into a structure will give you additional access to wisdom!

SURRENDERING TO
THE PROCESS

Everyone contains all the potential of the universe. Through dreaming, one connects to the true self and recognizes the potential she is here to actualize. However, only through embodying and *living* that recognition can the knowingness become wisdom and be fully experienced.

Like a woman giving birth to her first child, the dreaming woman, when she first begins to explore the vastness of her dreaming, is overwhelmed. The idea of being able to create a baby in your stomach is incomprehensible. The idea of being able to dream the world is immense.

At some point, however, the physiology of the labor takes over and there is nothing left but to give birth. So it is with dreaming. At a certain point, one realizes that she is a dreamer, and there is nothing to do but surrender to the work and give it livingness.

I give you these teachings and words with the love of my own dreaming in hopes that they will assist you in your dreaming. Let these dream teachings be your midwife!

PART TWO

DREAM CIRCLE:
AN ANCIENT FORM

The first dreamer was also the one being dreamed.

Consequently, all of life is simply made up of

a healing state that is dreaming itself beyond itself.

JOSEPH RAEL (BEAUTIFUL PAINTED ARROW)
Being and Vibration

"A healing state that is dreaming itself beyond itself." Those are beautiful, powerful words. The dream work is just that: a healing state. The healing of dreaming creates a unity and wholeness that calls us to work together as circles of dreaming healers.

The dream teachings along with the dream-circle work have truly changed the way each member of our circles lives her life. It opens ways of perceiving and interacting with the world, ways of healing the world, which enhance the multiple dimensionality of True Life.

In the following chapters I describe the specifics of the dream circle, an ancient ceremonial form designed to take dreamers into direct contact with their souls. I offer you a glimpse into the world of dreaming and healing.

5

The Dream Circle

The goal of the community is to make sure that each member of the community is heard and is properly giving the gifts that they have brought to this world.

SOBONFU E. SOME
The Spirit of Intimacy

African shamans Malidoma and Sobonfu Some speak eloquently in their books and conferences about the power of the African village. They encourage Western-ers to re-create the village in our highly modern lives so that we may feel the support of community. Sobonfu calls community "the spirit, the guiding light of the tribe, whereby people come together in order to fulfill a specific purpose, to help others fulfill their purpose, and to take care of one another."

I've always longed for my tribe. "Where are my people?" I've often asked.

Several years ago, I walked into my favorite esoteric book-store and saw a book called *Queen of Dreams* by Heather Valencia. I snapped it up, hardback prices notwithstanding, and read it hungrily in one sitting. After I finished, I felt as though I could fly. I had found another sister, one of my people, a woman who understood dreaming in the same way I did—only more. I could hardly wait to meet her.

I sat in a dream circle with Heather a few weeks later. She was masterful. She responded as though each dream were a direct message from spirit. Her approach to dreaming inspired me to listen deeply and hear dreams as divine events rather than shadow-filled psychological dramas.

I saw the incredible potential of a dream circle, a "village," if you will, that consistently gathers and deeply listens to one another. A dream circle makes sure each member is heard and supports each member's soul path, as Sobonfu Some so beautifully describes in her book.

Dreaming, in Heather's Native American tradition, is an act of encountering parallel universes in the realms of potential that exist on the Dream Weave. When I was with Heather, it was a homecoming. I *remembered* that night! Heather introduced me to my life's work—she showed me my dance on the Dream Weave, initiated me, and I remembered who I Am.

At the end of the meeting, someone asked, "Does anyone have a dream circle in town here?" I raised my hand. I took about thirty names and numbers home that night. I looked at my schedule, and it was already full to the brim with women's groups, art, children, husband, private clients, and me. I made choices about what to cancel, eliminate, and quit. Then I began a dream circle. My village began to take form.

WHAT IS A DREAM CIRCLE?

A dream circle is an ancient form that gives structure to the "work" of dreaming. The dreamers meet on a regular basis to share individual dreams. Each dreamer, one by one, speaks her dream to the circle. Then, each member of the circle mirrors the dream back to the dreamer by giving her information, feedback, and facts that she may not have known. We learn in circle that our dreams are indeed not individual but that we are all dreaming together, and our dreams fit together like puzzle pieces. Only through circle work do we get clear pictures of ourselves and our collective futures.

The dream-circle form comes to us from our female ancestors. Men have not traditionally involved themselves in dream circles. Men do not necessarily dream differently, but our Western socialization dictates that they think linearly. Because men do not have menstrual periods, it is difficult for them to connect with cyclical living and thinking, and therefore, it is more difficult for men to participate in the circle process. There are, of course, exceptional cases where men live in communities that support their connection with the cyclical nature of life, or they cultivate careers that allow them full access to dreamtime. These examples are for the most part exceptions in Western society. In my circles, we do have meetings with men from time to time, but in general, the circles are composed of women.

Women, because of their internalness, are natural dreamers. They have wombs; they have visions. Women and dreaming go hand in hand. Because of the hidden nature of their wombs and visions, women cannot see themselves clearly without being mirrored by others. Mirroring occurs in beautiful, healthy ways in dream circle; a woman shares her dream and listens as her trusted sisters speak of the energies the dream brings forth. As Heather describes it, the dreamer presents an ordinary-looking pebble in the form of a dream, and she receives a priceless gem in return. Each facet of the gem is polished by one of her dreaming sisters. Women are so mysterious, magical, and multidimensional that their ability to see their own totality is virtually non-existent. Dream circles are the mirrors in which we see ourselves clearly, fully, whole-ly, and holy.

WHY DREAM CIRCLES
ARE IMPORTANT

We lose our overview of life's mystery in the everyday world. Through reconnection with Great Dreamer and the mirrors held by dreaming sisters, we see the mystery of life again. Sitting in circle, hearing each other's dreams, and discovering that we are all dreaming together allows us to reconnect with mystery. When we leave circle, we return to traffic, the noise of the household or workplace, and the bills. Miraculously, the mystery connection remains and grows. Previously ignored synchronicities and coincidences become gifts from Great Dreamer, constantly reminding us that we are all partners in this divine game. Mundanity becomes Divinity.

Do not confuse the mirroring process that takes place in circle meetings with the familiar social practice of women looking to each other for approval, comparison, or criticism. Dream circle, rather, is an experience where loving sisters show aspects of dreaming to one another and tread the dream-dimension territory fearlessly. When a woman comes to circle with a disturbing dream she had about an animal, she is supported for her wildness. When a dreamer brings in a dream about a snake, circle reminds her that the Goddess often takes the form of the serpent to bring messages to her priestesses. The mirrors held by dreamers are the mirrors of mystery, power, magical transformation, and manifestation.

Humility is important in the dream-circle process. The temptation to become arrogant is sometimes present. Webster defines *arrogance* as "pride which exalts one's own importance." If a dreamer's pride interferes with her ability to accurately mirror, or see into the mirror of a dream, she throws the work of dreaming into a low and not particularly useful psychological dynamic.

However, humility and low self-esteem are not synonyms. Low self-esteem is the same as pride, only backwards. Humility is balance, an alignment with pure consciousness, and therefore humility cancels out either end of the spectrum. It is just as arrogant to think too lowly of oneself as it is to think too highly. Arrogance damages a circle. In dream circle, we want authenticity.

To be authentic is to be centered and in integrity with truth. An authentic being is neither flattered by compliments nor hurt by insulting remarks. She is neither inflated nor depressed by the truthful understanding of dream images. When a martial artist assumes a relaxed, albeit powerful position called *horse stance*, he is simultaneously at rest and alert to the energies around him. Authenticity is the dreamer's horse stance.

DREAM CIRCLES ARE THE MOUTH OF THE CAVE

When you look into a mirror, you know on some level that you are seeing the reverse reflection of yourself. However, the apparent accuracy of the reflection convinces you that you are seeing the real thing. When we look at our dreams without our sisters, we look into a reverse mirror. As dreamers, we *must know* when we are seeing in reverse.

Remember Plato's analogy of people in a cave who stood between the fire and the back wall watching their shadows dance? The people believed that the shadows were accurate representations of the world. Because of the echo in the cave, any sound that came from the outside circled around and seemed to come from the wall of shadows, reinforcing the belief that the wall was reality. One man ventured to the other side of the fire. They called him crazy. When he went to the mouth of the cave, he turned around to tell everyone they were looking in the wrong direction. The people refused to follow his advice. As in Plato's time, our commitment to what we believe is almost unbendable, even when we learn that what we believe is the reverse experience of truth.

When the dreamer first falls into sleep and relaxes the self-consciousness that ties her to the mundane world, she directly experiences the energy of the dimension of truth. Later, her mind puts symbols and pictures to the experience to "make sense" of it and help her remember the message. Depending on the dreamer's state of mind, and that of the collective, the symbols and pictures may be "light" or "dark." Either way, the images represent a basic principle of truth as experienced in that moment.

The dream circle's job is to stand at the mouth of the cave and recognize when the dreamer is dreaming a reversal and when the dreamer is dreaming a more direct aspect of truth.

OPENING A DREAM CIRCLE

Let's look at the practical aspect of running a dream circle. Heather Valencia taught me the basic form as it is practiced in indigenous circles around the world. Through personal experience and my own dreaming, I have slightly altered Heather's method.

Several dreamers come together, sit in a circle, and share dreams. They meet promptly at a preset time. My circles usually meet on Monday nights (Moon Day). How often per month your group meets is up to you. A circle that can meet first thing in the morning has a unique energy. But morning meetings are rare. They may be possible when on retreat, but morning meetings are not easy to organize in the fast-paced lifestyle most of us lead.

In a dream-circle meeting, first we ceremonially set the space. We use sage, drumming, meditation, visualization—various forms of opening the door to altered consciousness. We also light several candles so that no artificial light entraps us in ordinary consciousness. The goal of dream circle is to move into womb consciousness. Dream circle is a time when we see the dream lines that extend out of the abdomen and connect to the Weave. During dream circle, we open the eyes and ears of the womb so that collective dreaming energy, rather than a dreamer's personal ego, determines the meeting's flow.

THE LANGUAGE OF THE DREAM

In her book, Heather reminds us that nothing moves until there is sound: "Only when there was sound did life begin to move, dancing to the original, sweet music." Therefore, we speak our dreams to each other. The language of the dream makes dream circle a unique experience for most participants. Although psychological terms are familiar to most of us, this kind of vocabulary limits our ability to speak the dream.

I must stress here that our dream work is *not* psychological in nature. Dream circle is not a time of dream analysis, dream interpretation, or dream dialogue. Instead, dream circle is a time of speaking dream language from an awakened dreaming body and hearing the dreams of others with awakened dreaming ears. It is a time for dreamers to hear and speak from their bellies.

The Inuits, an Alaskan Native tribe, have no first-person singular pronoun in their language. Everything they utter is a collective statement. Inuit language would be an ideal language for dream circle. Despite the fact that our dreams are reported in the singular, understanding the dream as a collective experience is the first step toward understanding the language of the dream. The language of the dream is a collective patterning seen through dream eyes. Dream language is the language of consciousness. We speak this language authentically only when we remember that dreaming is not a personal event.

When you respond to a dream in circle, tell the dreamer the energies that the dream images evoke for you. Tell her ancient mysteries. Tell her about the deep connections you felt while she was telling the dream. Remind her of the secret animal behaviors in her dream. Give the dreamer information she might not have regarding the nature of colors or sounds in the dream. Speak to her as if her dream were a message from the collective soul to the circle. Act as if the whole circle were one soul cluster, gathered together to whisper reminders about each other's soul intent. Speak divine words to your sisters.

As you read the dreams shared in the rest of this book, pay attention both to their wording and to the wording of the dream-circle responses. You will see that although we use English and the first-person singular, we really speak a universal language that is symbolic and inclusive in nature.

THE DREAMING STONE

In a dream-circle meeting, as each person shares a dream she holds a dream stone. This stone, chosen by the circle, carries the energy and memory of their collective dreaming. You can use any stone. However, in North America the most powerful dream stones are uncut blue crystals, like raw aquamarine. Use the same stone week after week, year after year.

The purpose of the stone is threefold. First, the stone incorporates the Native American practice of using a talking stick when sitting in council. If you are holding the stone, you are holding the talking stick. Therefore, it is your responsibility to speak truthfully and clearly. If you are not holding the stone, it is your responsibility to listen unconditionally, without judgment, and with the ears of dreaming.

Second, because stones are the great holders, the dream-circle stone literally holds the energy of the dreaming. When you take a dreaming stone into your hand, the eye in the palm of your hand opens, and the energy in the stone penetrates your consciousness. The more the stone circulates, the greater the stone's power will be to awaken ancient memory in the circle.

Third, the stone carries the energy of the dreaming spiral round and round the circle, amplifying the energy as it moves. As circle members share and respond to dreams, the stone may pass through your hand as many as a dozen times in one night. Each time you take the stone, you will feel that its energy has magnified and you are being drawn to a "higher" place.

SHARING THE DREAMS

The dreamers pass this stone in a counterclockwise direction around the circle. The first time the stone moves around the circle, each person may share a dream, including the dream's date and the moon's placement when the dream occurred. After hearing many dreams in succession, the dreamers relax into a dreaming frame of mind. They have heard a preview of the evening.

The shared dream may be any dream—waking or sleeping, distant past or recent. The power of dream-circle work is in speaking the dream. Often, circles find that they are dreaming together just by listening to each other's dreams. Hearing familiar symbols and visions from the mouth of another creates a bond. We learn that we are not dreaming alone. We learn about the interconnectedness of all beings.

It is not necessary for every person to share a dream. The value of the sacred witness cannot be overstressed. Sometimes people sit in silence the entire night and still find the dream-circle experience to be very nurturing. Sometimes people will not share a dream but will participate through responses. Silence is not rude in dream circle.

After the initial round, the first person who shared a dream holds the stone and tells her dream again. Then she passes the stone to her right. The second person holds the stone and responds to the first dream. Next the second dreamer passes the stone to her right, and so on and so on. When the stone has made a full circle and everyone who wishes has commented on the first dream, the stone goes to the next woman and she shares her dream again. After each person has responded to the second dream, the third woman shares her dream again. On and on this pattern goes until all the dreams are complete.

In dream circle, we never correct each other. Someone may have heard "red shoes" when the dreamer actually said "green shoes." It does not matter. The sister who heard "red shoes" heard with the ears of her womb, so we let her speak about red shoes. The red shoes may be a message for one of us! The dreamer who heard "red shoes" is not consciously twisting her sister's dream—most women are totally unaware they have misheard a fact—rather, she is sharing a deep stirring within her dreaming space. Remember, dream circle is not dream analysis. Dream circle is speaking the language of the dream together under a very holy energetic field.

Usually, the dreamer does not comment on her own dream. She listens deeply and silently makes the inner connections helpful to her, but she remains aware that the dream is her gift to the circle. Sometimes, when all the other dreamers have spoken, she will briefly thank the circle or validate some of the statements.

THE COUNTERCLOCKWISE DIRECTION

The stone moves in a counterclockwise direction. For some, this is called the shamanic direction. It is the direction of the galactic spin—the direction the earth rotates and the direction the earth moves around the sun. Counterclockwise is also the direction the moon moves around the earth, the direction the Milky Way spirals, and the direction of the DNA helix. Counterclockwise is the feminine spiral, the spiral of the great nurturing darkness in which the galaxy exists. Remember, out of this darkness comes all potential, and the dream is potential given form.

The more times the stone moves around the circle, the more powerful the dreaming becomes. The counterclockwise spiral sends the dreamers' consciousness into the galactic realms. The comments from the circle elevate toward higher states of consciousness as the evening evolves.

Often, if the spiral becomes strong enough, several dreamers will dream together that night. Sometimes the circle energy will be so great that one of the dreamers will actually follow one of her dream lines all the way to the Great Dreamer. She will experience a Big Dream—a dream that gives vital information to the circle.

This spiraling of the circle is much more meaningful than it seems. Attention to the movement of the stone is very important during a dream-circle meeting. Some behaviors damage the energy of the spiral: passing the stone in the wrong direction, dialoguing across the circle, speaking out of turn, or making an egotistical comment. Damaged energy may jolt the dreamers out of their highly expanded consciousness. You know when you are almost asleep and then jolt back into waking? That is the same kind of jolt a dreamer receives when someone misuses energy during a circle. *If someone is holding the stone, no one else is to talk*. If you have already passed the stone and need to add something else to your statements, wait until everyone else has spoken and then raise your hand before the circle moves to the next dream. That will signal the dreamers to pass the stone to you again. *Do not reverse the direction of the flow*.

Remember, everyone is in an altered and vulnerable state. Your dream lines are out! It is imperative that the energy be kept clean and the flow remain continuous.

THE HUMILITY OF DREAMING

There are also other challenges that may occur during dream circle. Jealousy, spitefulness, lack of generosity, and competition are damaging to the relationships of dreamers. There is absolutely no room for these emotions and reactions in dream circle. These are social and behavioral patterns established when women and children were seen as possessions instead of powerful beings. Those patterns no longer apply, and they certainly do not serve the circle. If you allow these patterns in your dream circle, you will hurt yourself—literally and physically. You will experience pain in your womb.

The women of a dream circle must be mature. They must be able to correctly identify inappropriate behavior and be willing to speak the truth. They must be free of fear so that they will not hold back thoughts because they fear rejection or being wrong. Dream circle is a delicate balance, and a balance that only a woman of power can handle.

Practice in a dream circle helps one learn the humility of dreaming. What dreamers say regarding a dream will fit perfectly when everyone is humble and truthful. Words will upset, annoy, or inflate the dreamer if anyone is not humble. Practice in a dream circle also helps the dreamer learn whether she is dreaming the shadow or the light. When someone "sees" the mouth of the cave through the images of a dream, everyone benefits.

The work of dreamtime is difficult. One person cannot do it alone. It requires the energy of a group. This is why we dream in circles.

CLOSING THE CIRCLE

After completing all the dreams, it is time to close the circle for the night. Closing the circle is extremely important.

The energy must remain so that the dreamers may carry it into dreamtime. However, people have to drive or negotiate the journey home, so they must come back from their altered state.

We usually "slide" out of circle. We stop and say thank you to each other. We put the stone away so that it doesn't influence us any longer. We blow out the candles and turn on some soft lights to change the energy. We visit casually about mundane, meaningless things. As each woman reaches a sense of being "normal" (whatever *that* means), she slowly gathers her things to leave. Often we judge whether someone is ready to leave by how long it takes her to find her keys!

As you leave a circle, you will realize that more happened than you consciously registered. You will sense a difference in your walk and feel as if your organs have been massaged. You will know that women are dreaming a new way of being, and you have just integrated that new way through an experience of deep community. You will know and understand more deeply after a good, restful sleep. Sweet dreams!

6

● ● ● ● ● ● ● ● ● ● ● ● ● ● ●

How Dream Circle
Changes Your Life

*Dreams often inwardly align us and when we share dreams within a group we share
this inner alignment and have it reinforced by others. In this way we work together,
helping each other and creating a group space where the outer and inner are aligned.*

LLEWELLYN VAUGHAN-LEE
In the Company of Friends

Finding your dream circle is like finding your soul cluster.
Your dream-circle members see your divinity—your
potential self. They are not particularly interested in
your psychology. They are interested in your sacred reason for
living. They support your patterns and your changing of
patterns. They mirror to you your soul self. Your life becomes a
process of faith, spiritual flow, continuity from source to self,
and connection to community.

There are plenty of places in our society where one can go
for analysis, guidance, counseling, support-group dynamics,

criticism, or a make-over. In fact, many dream-circle sisters belong to such groups or have a therapist. Part of dream-circle work is to keep the psychology and personality of the dreamer clean and clear, for only then can dreams soar to other heights.

Dream circle is a place where women see each other for their divinity. Dream circle is sacred. Dream circle provides a unique arena for people, because the energy of the dynamic is holy. Dream circle is a place of worship.

DREAM CIRCLES ARE TODAY'S ANCIENT TEMPLES

Scholars such as Merlin Stone and Maria Gimbutas give us vast information about the matristic temples of ancient Europe. Lorre Goodrich, one of the foremost scholars on ancient Celtic civilizations, speaks eloquently about Avalon and similar schools of training. Elinor Gadon, in her book *The Once and Future Goddess*, discusses temples in great detail. She includes descriptions of the sleeping (dreaming) chambers and pictures of some sculptures of dreaming women.

Evidence indicates that in ancient societies when particularly talented dreamers were born, elder dreamers recognized them and taught them from a very early age how to be master dreamers. In the Euro-goddess civilizations, there were apparently temples where little dreamers as young as three or four went to live. Raised to be dreamers, taught to know dreaming, and trained to live in full integrity with the Weave, dreaming priestesses lived very different lives from modern women. Society honored dreams and sought counsel from them.

Many people of our generation were born into what pop psychology calls "dysfunctional families," ranging from alcoholism, sexual abuse, racial hatred, emotional abuse, or misogyny. Many of us are actually self-identified and defined by our particular brand of childhood abuse. "I'm an adult child of an alcoholic." "I'm an incest survivor." "I was the victim of ceremonial abuse." These are phrases often uttered in the privacy of my counseling sessions. Most women respond with a long deep stare into my eyes, a huge sigh of relief, and then tears when I say, "I do not know a woman of power who didn't experience unspeakable pain in her childhood."

We were born into the reversal of the dream—in the back of the cave. We learned how *not* to be fully alive, and our commitment to the status quo of that reversal may keep us only partially alive. We've mastered the shadow dance. Now we are being called to the fire. Today's dreaming temple is an inner temple. It first activates in the deepest self, and then hopefully the actualized dreamer finds her circle.

Consciousness has changed since those ancient temple days. Dreamers have taken other paths and chosen to actualize other kinds of potentials. Today, in order to become a mature, schooled dreaming master, one has to teach herself. The dreamer has to lose memory of who she is, use enormous will to remember again, and then surrender to the humility of dreaming and being dreamed. It is an amazingly powerful process. I know this because I have done it, as have most of the women in my dream circles. I invite you to join us.

WHY WE NEED DREAM CIRCLES

Over the past few thousand years, the illusion of separation has prevailed in our living and our dreaming. We have believed that we live and dream as individuals and that our connection to community results from conscious choices to

interact with and influence others. We believe that inter-
action with and influence over others are forms of power.
This is not true.

Separation is the very illusion that keeps us from our
power. While separation may be beneficial for scientific investigation or technological development, the *belief* in separation
distorts our vision of ourselves and the Dream Weave's divine
perfection. Believing that the human personality instigates
thought and action apart from a universal wholeness is the
misunderstanding that creates evil. By working in dream circles, women are able to study dreams as the beginning of form
and to understand the Dream Weave as the perfection from
which all thought, action, and manifestation originates. That
is the power of the dream circle.

Dream circle changes your life because it trains you to see
yourself as divine and inseparable from the world and the
whole universe. It reminds you to look for ideas of separation
and weed them out of your experience. Dream circle calls you
to your soul. Knowing that once a week, or even once a
month, your circle sees you as a soul bearing sacred gifts and
divine words changes the way you walk your ordinary day.
Dream circle helps you see others as divine beings.

HOW TO FIND YOUR CIRCLE

Ask for your circle and pray for your sisters to make themselves known to you. Start a dream journal and chart your
dreams. Talk to others about dreaming. You know the phrase
"When the student is ready, the teacher will come." Well, I say,
"When the dreamer is ready, the circle will form."

A dream circle may take a long time to gel. People will
come and go for no apparent reason. Some members will

want to dominate and control. The energy of dream circle will not allow these people to stay. In eight years, I have asked only one woman to leave the circle. On occasion, people have brought inappropriate energy to the circle; however, relatively soon they just stopped coming. No one had to speak to them about leaving. The energy of a dreaming circle is so divine, so subtle, and so holy that misfitting, aggressive, and needy energies just do not stick.

As a rule of thumb, we allow anyone who expresses desire to come to a circle. We ask new members to observe the first one or two sessions. If the new members feel drawn to do the work, they begin to come regularly and participate fully. We don't worry about "protection." The spiraling nature of the circle's energy just seems to spin the right people in and the wrong people out. When a member leaves, we bless them. If they want to come back, we bless that too. Remember that the energy of the circle is at work, not the personalities of the dreamers.

WHAT IS THAT ENERGY?

The energy aroused during a dream circle comes from a consciousness that exists behind the scenes. It is the gear that runs the wheel of life. However, many people are not aware of the energetic system beyond everyday life.

In this book, the term *dreaming* refers to a deep awareness that exists in sleeping and waking. It is an awareness of the subtle realms of consciousness—a knowingness beyond obvious information. Dreaming is a shamanic way of understanding everyday occurrences. The energy that penetrates a dream circle stirs as the counterclockwise flow guides the dreamers into a galactic, cyclical, and cosmic consciousness. Subatomic physicists tell us that if we had microscopes powerful enough to penetrate all the way to the nucleus of an atom, we would eventually see nothing but vibration. Dream circle functions as that microscope—the energy of the dream circle is the subtle vibration of life.

When one goes to sleep, one goes into a pre-dreaming contact with the energy on the dimension of truth. That kind of energy re-creates itself in dream circle if the participants are able to connect to the womb lines and disconnect from personal will. Dream-circle energy is like our between waking and sleeping energy when sounds, smells, and vibrations are amplified. The energy of dream circle must be honored deeply and tended carefully.

How do we honor and tend to the energy? We ignore it while being acutely aware of it. We honor and tend the energy by treating it gingerly. We laugh and point out paradox, irony, and high humor in dreams. We maintain a lightness of being and take nothing too seriously. Piety slips in easily if everyone is serious. However, we simultaneously miss *nothing*. Every bird that chirps outside, every candle that flickers, every dog that barks, and every phone that rings happens for specific reasons around the dreaming energy.

THE ENERGY CHANGES YOUR LIFE

What we say in circle about dreams is important. However, our words are profoundly superficial compared to the energetic experience we have in circle. Bathing in the force field of the energy is really what makes the change in your life.

Dream circle is ceremony, power, and holy energy. When you allow your atoms to be regenerated by the energy, allow

yourself to breathe the experience, and allow yourself to connect with others in that environment, you literally change
your experience of yourself.

DREAM CIRCLE CHANGES
YOUR RELATIONSHIPS

It is a woman's nature to be a social person. Relationship is a
woman's realm. Most women will sell out their integrity to
make a relationship work. If they believe that being a powerful
dreamer will jeopardize a relationship, some women will
choose to limit their power. For that reason, the hardest thing
a woman will ever do is free herself from her social limitations
and move into dreaming. Yet after she frees herself, she sees
that dreaming is the only way to truly live.

Regular dream-circle attendance brings a new understanding to the dreamer. All of our lives we have used precious
energy to avoid alignment with forces we perceived as disrup-
tive to the status quo. Each wall we created to block awarenesses of the subtle realms required enormous personal
energy. It has exhausted us. Sitting in dream circle removes
those walls for a few hours. As a result, the heart opens and
dissolves the resistance to wholeness. One feels rested, ener-
gized, and restored.

The result of this restored energy shows up most profoundly in relationships. One woman came to me shortly
after she started attending circle. She was afraid that the new
openings and ideas learned in dream circle would damage her
marriage. She could not imagine that her husband could
accept her new experiences as anything but "woo-woo" and
crazy. She felt that the dreamer's path led her directly away
from her marriage.

We looked at her soul contract (astrological chart) and compared it to her husband's. It was obvious that they already walked two different paths. Those paths were not necessarily contradictory, but they were very different. "How can it harm your marriage to be more clear about your soul's intent?" I asked. It was as simple as that. She went home and all is well.

Every relationship strengthens as each person discovers his or her own life path more clearly. We are not separate units. Our paths are interdependent but not codependent or independent. Dream circle helps us understand the interrelatedness, or relationship, of all thought, action, and potential. Dream circle empowers us to be fully present in our relationships by making us more fully available to the deeper understandings and connections in life.

DREAM CIRCLE CHANGES YOUR COMMUNITY LIFE

In addition to changing our understandings and insights of personal relationships, dream circle also dramatically changes our perspective of the community and the earth.

Our beloved Mother Earth goes through many changes: earthquakes, volcanoes, floods, and fires. As we have observed and integrated these changes in dream circle, we have learned that sometimes we have prior knowledge of them through dreaming. How we integrate that knowledge and what we do with it have become important aspects of our work. The following example taught us a profound lesson regarding the connections between dreaming, the earth, and our community of brothers and sisters.

Earthquake People

Connie

☽ void

There was an earthquake in the city. People were standing on building ledges preparing to jump. It seemed an odd response.

Heather gathered six dreamers. She asked each of us to jump into the cold pool behind my house one at a time and to come back up and make one statement that had come into our minds while under water. All our statements together equaled the "dream." The purpose was to fully understand what was happening to our brothers and sisters that made them react so unreasonably.

The first sister dived in. She came back up and said, "The concrete crackles..."

I was second. I did a dive off the side. I came back up: "Great slices of the Earth open to reveal a whole civilization of beings living in the fault lines below."

I didn't stay around to hear what else was said. Instead I went down into the faults.

All the fault lines under the city—and there are hundreds—opened up about two feet wide and thirty feet deep. I met a civilization of beings who lived there. They were in charge of planning the quakes. I saw the computerized central nervous system of the Earth. Earthquake beings calculated the timing and power of the quakes based on the stress needs of the Earth. They also factored in the effect a quake would have on the people. They were trying to figure out how they had miscalculated the response of the population in this particular case.

In this dream, we saw that when Mother Earth opens her teachings to the dreamer, it is the dreamer's responsibility to accept that gift joyfully and immediately. If the dreamer had stayed to hear what the other people "saw" as they jumped into the pool, she would have missed meeting an entire civilization of people: our mineral-kingdom partners on this planet.

Mother Earth is a sentient and intelligent being. She is taking her needs and the needs of her children into calculation at all times. We are working in partnership with her during this time of planetary change.

A few days after that dream, the Los Angeles Rebellion broke out in reaction to the "not guilty" verdict in the Rodney King beating trial. The rebellion deeply disturbed many members of our circle. We met to discuss what we could do for the community. During the discussion, we realized that many aspects of the dream had manifested; most specifically, people were reacting to the loss of control in very bizarre and irrational ways.

By blending the waking community consciousness with the deeper levels of community consciousness we had learned from the dream, we saw hope in a situation that many people in the city experienced with fear, horror, and hopelessness. Through what we call energy wisdom, that day the dream circle saw the rebellion fires as a necessary purification. We saw Los Angeles as a partner to other countries and cities in the world where major changes were occurring—Russia, South Africa, and Central America. It was as if Los Angeles had become the lid on Mother Earth's pressure cooker, and by letting off steam, the stress in the rest of the world would also be released.

We felt that this dream had sent us this message: We can *dream* ourselves through the world's changes and into new dimensions of being. By trusting the process, knowing we are communicating and interfacing with Mother Earth's sentience, and remembering that all energy is conscious energy, we can dream hope into the most devastating-looking circumstances.

The rebellion died down after three days of chaos. The next morning, dream circle joined thousands of other neighbors armed with push brooms, shovels, and garbage bags to clean up South Central. We knew that the action was a tiny reflection of the greater truth that the rebellion had eased the earth's stress levels. We also knew that new energies were now at work.

In Southern California, we live with earthquakes, fires, floods, and human violence. Our dream circle has learned that by listening carefully to each other's dreams, charting them, and awakening to the deeper messages in them, we can predict when something profound is about to happen. We have also learned that the fear most people experience during violent events actually increases the level of tragedy. We work in dreaming and our daily lives to prepare appropriately, support each other, and hold an attitude of calm trust.

Our personal experiences of the "acts of God du jour," as we have come to call them, are not filled with tragedy but with change and growth. Our emotions are not sourced in fear but in faith. We are actively and consciously choosing to manifest an option from the Dream Weave that allows us inner peace.

Peace changes our relationship to our community. We feel prepared and inspired to help others stay calm and meet daily experiences with hope, faith, and joy.

DREAM CIRCLE CHANGES YOUR LIFE

Dream circle changes your life because your connection with life changes. Your life changes because your mind changes. Your life changes because you no longer believe in separation. Your life changes because you dream the changes.

7

Dreaming as a Spiritual Practice

Dreams are the original language of the spiritual path. . . . Dreams are a straight connection to the divine heart of the cosmos.

ROSEMARY ELLEN GUILEY
Dreamwork for the Soul

A spiritual practice is our rudder as we sail through life. In modern days with all the hubbub of urbanity, a spiritual practice is an absolute necessity, although few people really understand that. As we fly down the information highway, stopping periodically to honor the magic and power of life is paramount. In one of his books, *Journey to Ixtlan*, Carlos Castaneda's teacher, don Juan, told him that there is no other task in our entire lives which is more important than the purification of our spirits: "Lowering his voice to almost a whisper, he said that if I really felt that my spirit was distorted I should simply fix it—purge it, make it perfect—because there was no other task in our entire lives which is more important."

For some, the idea of a spiritual practice is frightening. For others, the suggestion that one needs a spiritual practice brings great resistance and back-turning. It need not. Spiritual practice is simply the pathway one uses to travel through the wonder called life. We need a conscious spiritual practice in order to walk that pathway in integrity with our deepest understanding of the wonder. We need to consciously make choices that reflect our cosmology—our universal philosophy.

The truth is, you have a philosophy whether you know it or not. It is either a conscious philosophy you have carefully investigated, polished, honed, and sculpted according to your heart's truth, or it is a philosophy that society has handed to you. In this day and age, it is highly recommended that you become conscious of your inner cosmology, because society's values may be slipping!

If you are living in a way that does not reflect your deepest beliefs and understandings, you may simply be distracting yourself. You may be allowing something other than truth to govern your life. You may be contributing to a social cosmology that is no longer serving the greater whole.

Dreaming is a practice like many spiritual practices. Dreaming, as a spiritual practice, complements and augments any other spiritual practice you may already have, or it can stand on its own. Dreaming requires impeccable behavior on the part of the participant. In fact, it demands a higher level of integrity than some of the more worldly spiritual systems because the dreamer crosses many otherworldly dimensions.

In ordinary consciousness, we live in a polarized reality. Everything in the three-dimensional world that we call "real" has an opposite. Everything is magnetically charged to attract its opposite. We live in a mirror world. That is not the case in dreaming realities. In dreaming, we are on the other side of the mirror. Polarities dissolve and suddenly we attract what is *like* us. Dreaming-dimension dynamics pull us toward that which empowers us—that which *is* us.

For this reason, the dreamer must enter dreaming realities in a spirit of the sacred. Entering a dream is like entering a church or sanctuary. We must be clean in mind, body, and emotion. Our relationship with our souls must be intact. This way, we can trust that what we magnetize in a dream will be of the highest benefit to ourselves as well as to all beings and dynamics.

From the beginning of my work in dreamtime, I learned from my teachers to follow the four sacred paths of a dreamer: physical, mental, emotional, and soul.

THE PHYSICAL PATH

When you prepare to go into dreamtime, the first thing you do is alter your awareness. Physically, that involves switching your relationship with gravity (magnetic pull) from the vertical to the horizontal plane. The act of lying down automatically readjusts your body workings, changes your relationship to Mother Earth, and prepares you for the soul journey.

The first aspect of the physical path, then, involves daily attention to body needs at bedtime. The dreamer must learn what kinds of foods and liquids to consume in the evening in order to allow the body its best rest. This practice is highly personal. There is no "dreamer's diet." I know, for example, that if I go to bed with alcohol in my system, my dreaming is going to be different—more labored and difficult—than if I go to bed with water in my system. I know that a heavy meal "drugs" me, and the energies I magnetize in dreaming will be denser and heavier. This is my pattern. It may or may not be yours.

It is important to be particularly attentive to food and exercise on a moon power day. *Remember, the moon power day occurs on the day of each month that the moon moves through the exact sign and degree it reflected at your birth.* Moon power days usually bring important dreams, and it is beneficial to be in a state of consciousness that allows the body to rest—not requiring it to process physical "stuff."

Some dreamers also set a stage for dreamtime by burning essential oils in a diffuser, creating a dream altar near the head of the bed, or using a dream bowl. Any of these actions can help the dreamer focus on the fact that she is about to move into a parallel dimension and that the journey is sacred.

The second aspect of the physical path involves movement during waking time. The dreamer comes out of sleep realizing that she's been traveling in her dream body. The dream body, of course, carries itself differently, because it has fewer limitations and restrictions than the waking body. The transition between the waking and dreaming bodies is extremely important. The first movements a dreamer makes upon awakening determine how the dreamtime journey will integrate with the waking reality. Most people simply jump out of bed, begin the hustle and bustle, and ignore the transition. This is physically jolting and unhealthy for a dreamer. Dreaming demands a level of conscious integration between the sleeping and waking bodies. The dream body must turn the power of movement over to the waking body with grace and dignity. Otherwise, the dreamer will walk in disorientation throughout the day.

Again, the movements one makes to create the transition between bodies are up to the individual. Some dreamers do stretching, some a tai chi form, and some use Reiki. Two dreamers in our circle have created a series of movements and chants based on the Jewish morning prayers, which they've documented in their book *Minding the Temple of the Soul*. The transition movements need not take long, but they need to be a part of the dreamer's morning ritual. The change of bodies—changing of the guard, if you will—is much more important than you can imagine. Part of what keeps us unaware of dreaming is the lack of communication between the sleeping and waking bodies.

The third aspect of the physical path involves noting the thirteen cycles of a dreamer's year. As mentioned in chapter 4, every woman has thirteen lunar cycles in her dreaming year. We learn from charting that certain times of a woman's cycle align her body with the moon—and therefore with specific types of dreaming. Physically, it is important to give special attention to your body during certain parts of your cycle. You must learn exactly which days of your cycle are most important to your dreaming.

By charting my dreams according to moon time, I have learned many interesting things about myself. For example: My most informative and prophetic dreams come a day or two before my flow begins. My prophetic timing is eighteen to twenty-one days. In other words, the prophecy will usually manifest within my next cycle time. This means that when I have a prophetic dream, I need to use my flow days to prepare for its manifestation. I almost never remember dreams on my third and fourth days of bleeding (heaviest bleeding time) and the twentieth to twenty-first days after bleeding (heaviest bloating time).

This kind of body awareness allows the dreamer a wider spectrum of understanding about the life force in general. Dreaming and working with dreams in relation to your body cycles literally changes your life. Studying dreams in relation

POWER-DAY
DREAMING
See page 68

to physical patterns helps you understand, love, and honor your body's multidimensionality.

The daily practices of watching your diet and gently waking your body, as well as the cyclical practice of tracking patterns and honoring your body rhythms, ultimately create healthy dreaming.

THE MENTAL PATH

Mentally, we keep ourselves strictly bound by our belief systems. We imprison ourselves by what we believe to be true, real, or possible. Dream work allows us to bypass our belief systems and move into the universal truth. However, a dreaming vocabulary is imperative for understanding the worlds in which we travel.

Phase one of the mental path is charting. By charting our dreams we actually train the mind to think in cycles and patterns. In school we learned to think linearly and syllogistically. Deductive and inductive reasoning are highly honored in the ordinary realities of our world. The dreamer, however, must also include thinking in circles.

Cyclical thinking moves one out of the everyday world of polarized forms and into the universal river of thought. The universal river of thought is a wheel, a cycle, a spiral, a Milky Way. The dreamer's mind must learn to track energetic spirals. Charting dreams and reading their patterns will change the way your mind works.

Charting may sound boring or seem like busywork. In some ways, it may be busywork. However, charting keeps your mental body occupied so that the universal river of thought can flow into your personal mind without being restricted by limited belief systems.

Phase two of the mental path involves training the mind to eliminate judgment. Of course, discrimination and decision making must remain intact, but holding opinions and judgments of people's actions and words will only throw the mind of the dreamer into a state of ordinariness that does not serve anyone.

Have you ever had a highly bizarre dream that seemed perfectly normal at the time? This is an example of how you can operate from the nonjudgment of a master dreamer's mental body. When your consciousness is in the highest dream states, there is no right or wrong. Dreaming is not about *doing*, it's about *being*. The dreaming mind tells you who you are, not what you should be doing. Unless you are able to travel back and forth between a dreaming mind and a socially programmed mind, you may complete your entire life without ever remembering who you are.

Practice allowing one part of your consciousness to see every action, every circumstance, and every event from the nonjudgmental dream mind's point of view. Soon you will be living with a mind that can experience a deeper meaning in every action, circumstance, and event. Then, when those sacred dreams come, you'll be able to read the messages because you will know the vocabulary of the universal mind. When prophetic dreams speak, you will be able to help create beneficial outcomes. First, however, you must discipline your mind so that the dreaming language develops.

THE EMOTIONAL PATH

The uniqueness of the human emotional system gives the emotional body enormous power. Because we are capable of assigning meaning, definition, and dimension to our life by coloring it with emotion, we hold a very special place in the universe of sentient beings. The mature person knows how to use the dynamics of emotion to create depth and beauty, richness and vision. Truly, nothing impacts and contours one's life like the emotional body. Even the most difficult life experiences can be gratifying for the person who knows how to run emotion toward the beauty end of the spectrum.

Emotional energy comes from the desire to be whole. When you feel emotion, you feel a surge of spiritual power calling you home. If you train yourself to always remember that the feeling of emotion is a spiritual calling, the charge and judgment you place on an emotional experience will transform, and emotion will become a sacred ally. You will realize that the only difference between ecstasy and fear is how your system judges the energy.

Emotional bondage to the past cripples. For most people, it is easier to overcome a physical or mental disability than an emotional disability. Ironically, we know this, yet we tend to make life choices that sustain harmful emotional patterns anyway. In our society, literally hundreds of psychological therapies are available because the emotional damage in many people is quite severe.

The dreamer has a special relationship to emotion. First, she knows that the emotional climate she brings into the dream greatly influences the dream's content and power. It is imperative that the dreamer's emotional energy be clean and clear when going to bed. The most powerful way that truth comes in dreamtime is through a dreamer's clean and available emotional body. If a dreamer has an emotional bias, the dream's message will be altered.

Second, the dreamer knows that she is a voyager into the great realm of possibility. She knows that when she moves into the realm of possibility, she will attract energies in accordance with her soul. The dreamer knows that she must be free and fully available to the adventure's power in order to experience the dream. Emotional crippling limits the experience and mobility of the dreamer.

Finally, dreaming requires energy. If the dreamer expends a high percentage of personal energy on the emotional dynamics of her waking life, she simply will not have enough energy available for her multidimensional life.

Let me be more direct. Every experience you have in life is interpreted through your emotional body. Some experiences attach themselves to you—you send an emotional fiber, an energetic extension cord, into the memory of that experience to keep it alive. The act of keeping a memory emotionally alive, whether it is a fond memory, a memory of abuse or victimization, or a relatively indifferent memory, saps your energy. Eventually, you will have so many emotional fibers holding memories alive that when a new experience comes similar to one you have already had, you will define it, label it, and tuck it away without allowing it the opportunity to express itself. Dreaming requires a clean emotional body. *We do not clean our emotional body in order to "forget" our history. We clean our body in order to be fully available to the present.*

The emotional path of the dreamer involves living in the gratitude principle at all times. The emotional energy of any waking or sleeping circumstance enhances and defines the experience. Living in the gratitude principle means continually expressing thanks for every moment of life. If you are living in gratitude, emotion will never imprison or limit your expression.

In order to have all your energy available, you must call it back. You must visualize pulling every emotional fiber back into your body and thereby restoring your energy.

The technique for restoring energy is breathing. It is similar to the practice of recapitulation taught to Carlos Castaneda by don Juan. Each day—preferably at night just before bed, but any time will do—sit quietly and breathe. As you breathe, allow every single memory of the past twenty-four hours to present itself as if you were watching a movie. Picture by picture and frame by frame, stop the action. Scan the emotions connected to the frozen picture in front of you. *Give thanks* for the experience, because it has made you the person you are. Then deeply inhale and pull all your emotional energy back from the picture. Next, intentionally exhale all attachments and release them into the picture. The picture will become sepia-toned or black-and-white and will lose dimension. When the picture looks like a photograph, you know you are successful. The memory of the experience is not lost, but now the emotional energy feeds you. The emotions are no longer sapping your energetic reservoir. If the picture is still in color or is still three-dimensional, breathe again until it changes. Then allow the movie to go to the next scene.

It may sound as if I am asking you to disconnect or disengage from life. However, I am asking quite the opposite. I am giving you a technique to ensure that all your energy will be available all the time so that you can fully engage and meaningfully connect with your dreaming as well as your waking life. If a high percentage of your emotional energy is tied up keeping your history alive, it is virtually impossible to be attentive to each moment as it unfolds before you.

In dreamtime, as in waking, if a good part of your emotional energy is invested in mundane reality, you inhibit your ability to move freely on the Dream Weave. *The energies you magnetize in dreaming will be the energies matching the emotional climate you carry into the dream.*

In the beginning, the technique for gaining full access to energy is quite demanding, because it is necessary to apply the gratitude principle to your history. You must call every memory up for investigation—every scene from your childhood, every entanglement with your mother or father, and every relationship with a lover. When you apply the gratitude principle to your whole life, you restore *all the energy* of your beingness.

As a result of practicing energy restoration, every day you will literally feel yourself becoming more alive. Every time you sit down and give thanks, you pull your life energy back and become more ecstatic. Life takes on a glow—a luminescence. Each moment comes to you in divine proportion and you become "addicted" to recovering your energy.

Try it! Give yourself the gift of emotional freedom. Trust yourself enough to let history live without sapping your sacred energy. You will not believe the change in your life, the change in how you are able to dream the world, the change in your earth dance.

After years of applying the gratitude principle to my life, I have found I practice the breathing technique almost constantly. When a client leaves my room, I pull my energy back. When I leave a dear friend, I pull my energy back as I drive away. When I have an argument, I pull my energy back immediately. The results are astounding. My need to win an argument dissolves, because my need to pay attention to the dynamic is more profound. I no longer need my friends' approval, because my need to experience truth and freedom is greater. My need for clients to "heal" or "become spiritual" disappears, because my only prayer is one of gratitude. At the end of the day, I have little left to do. Sometimes something historical will come up when I sit to contemplate, and sometimes my screen is blank. I like the blank times.

Then comes dreamtime. I move into the Weave gently—I travel freely to the places my soul longs to experience. I sleep knowing that I will magnetize goodness and beauty, because my essential self travels unburdened by fears and unhampered by emotional bondage. I bring back visions, information, and powers that cycle into my everyday life and reinforce my freedom and availability in the waking present.

The dreamer's emotional path is powerful and profound. Emotion defines every aspect of life, every dimension, every definition of reality. When emotions are free from historical bonds, the dreamer is free to dream a future of beauty and peace.

THE SOUL PATH

For the dreamer, prayer is the most important practice. This section is short, sweet, and simple. Pray. Like the physical path, prayer is highly personal. There is no "dreamer's prayer." Use whatever you know about prayer.

I will caution you not to use prayer to tell God what to do. Pray simply for your essential self to be present in every waking and sleeping moment. Pray that your consciousness will be pure and clean. Pray that communication with your soul will be continuous and unhampered. Pray for inner peace.

Soon you will find that prayer underscores every moment of your life. Gentle, loving prayer replaces the mental chatter that used to occupy your brain. Disturbing moments will be embraced with prayer. Phone calls will be punctuated with prayer. You will become a walking prayer.

Now I often find myself praying in dreams. Sometimes I stop off at a church in the middle of a relatively ordinary dream, light a candle, and say a prayer. For example, I remember once I dreamed that a bad man was chasing me. I ducked into a bathroom, lay down in the tub, and prayed—not for rescue or safety but for the expression of crystal-clear light. My pursuer completely dissolved in the light.

Prayerful communication with the Creator keeps your wiring and plumbing in tip-top shape. No matter what kind of light comes your way, you will be able to handle it. No matter what kind of refuse, you will be able to flush it. The prayerful dreamer is a holy being.

THE RESULTS OF A SPIRITUAL PATH

Practicing the paths of dreaming results in a continual re-creation of the dreamer. She lives in a charming spiral. The dreamer awakens in the morning and blends the beauty of her dream body into the power of her waking body through movement and song. She allows her mental body the privilege of viewing the cycle of life by writing down her dream. Then she charts her dream pattern as it relates to the great cycles of the stars, the heavens, and universal thought. She blends every action of her day with a constant underscoring of prayer. Then, just before returning to sleep, she reclaims all her emotional energy so that she can go into her dream body with a clean and clear soul alignment.

The dreamer is continually re-dreamed. Practicing the dreamer's four paths enables you to live your life with freedom of expression, a wide range of movement, and the vision of many dimensions. Your life will be full of grace.

PART THREE

RE-DREAMING:
HOW DREAMING CAN
ALTER YOUR PAST

"I have pledged myself to turn you into a wizard,"
Merlin began, *"and that is not achieved through a collection*
of useless potions and spells. If anything, you're already under
a spell that I must waken you from, the spell of time. True
wizards are not bound by it; we live in the past, present, and
future all at once. . . . People live their lives . . . along a narrow
path from past to present to future. When they come to the end
of their little petal, they die. But as wizards, we see the whole
flower. . . . Because we know the truth—that
we are existing in all times at once."

DEEPAK CHOPRA
The Return of Merlin

In his beautifully written novel, Deepak Chopra uses
Merlin's voice to describe many of the scientific and spiritual
truths the author teaches in his seminars. Replace *wizard*
with *dreamer* in this passage and you have a perfect
definition for a *Master Dreamer*.

The next few chapters describe how dreaming changes the past. My circles are re-dreaming what has been. They are moving beyond history into a collective truth. Most of the women did not see their dreams as re-dreaming history until they brought them to dream circle, because most of us are attached to believing that dreams are separate and unique representations of our own narrow path. In circle, we saw repeated patterns in our dreams. Suddenly the fearful and personally threatening symbols were transformed. Death, violence, snakes, and blackness—symbols defined by psychology as *the shadow*—now became collective messages of re-dreaming.

Society says that the past is concrete. "You can't change history." Yet the past I was taught in history class has most certainly been altered. The history of my own people and my country is not as pretty, godly, or altruistic as textbooks once indicated. What does that mean in light of what I now know?

The past is malleable, because infinite pasts exist, just as infinite futures exist. There is no one way to remember the past. What may have been abuse to the child turns out to be life-enforcing and strengthening for the self-actualized woman of power. Dreaming gives us access to a wider range of pasts.

8

Re-dreaming the Myth

The dragons that jealously guard the myth of dependency, the myth of female inferiority, and the myth of romantic love are fearsome opponents. This is not a journey for cowards.

MAUREEN MURDOCK
The Heroine's Journey

Maureen Murdock told me that she wrote *The Heroine's Journey*, in part, to help women reweave the myths that make up our web of belief. Reading Maureen's book for the first time was a profound experience because the book taught me that as dreamers we must rewrite our archetypal understandings—our mythology. In dream circle, women often re-dream myths and transform the dragons guarding the myths.

A myth is a story so firmly embedded into the Weave that it becomes a law of behavior. A myth is collective patterning that may or may not serve the individual's healthy evolution. In fact, for women, the mythologies of present societies are imprisoning and out of integrity with truth.

WHAT IS RE-DREAMING?

"Re-dreaming" can appear in several forms.

The first form of re-dreaming is when we change a myth in a dream. Often, we see mythological images and characters in a dream. Equally often, the dream does not quite follow the typical mythological story. The dreamer creates a slightly altered version of the myth in order to open the story to a wider interpretation or a more gentle influence over life.

A second way to re-dream is to go back to sleep (after awakening) or to take charge of the dream (by becoming lucid) and change the outcome of the dream. This sounds hard, but with a little practice, changing a dream is very simple, and the result is quite profound. Rewriting a nightmare is every dreamer's right. Freya, one of our circle members, taught this idea to her schoolchildren.

NOTE FROM FREYA

Last week I was in a classroom with third graders. We had finished discussing a shooting in a nearby school and how afraid the children now were to come to school. The teacher casually said, "They will probably all have nightmares tonight." I grabbed the opportunity and asked, "How many of you have nightmares?" Every hand in the room went up. "Well, did you know you can re-dream your dreams?" For the first time, I had the children's attention. I am now teaching dreaming to children! Even the teacher is excited about learning. I am so grateful for the opportunity to really give a child a tool that will assist him or her all through life.

Re-dreaming can take a third form when we change our understanding of a dream. Recurring dreams, or theme dreams, often repeat themselves to us because we haven't thoroughly understood them. This may be the result of interpreting one's own dreams. When a woman interprets her dreams without help from her circle, she will often use a socialized understanding of a symbol. Her interpretation, however, may actually perpetuate a misunderstanding of the symbol. For example, a dreamer may interpret a snake dream as fearful, as a temptation, or as an indication of sexual repression, depending on which myth she believes. If those snake dreams recur, it's probably because she hasn't understood the deeper message of the dream. Her circle will give her many new understandings of serpent power: the regenerative nature of the snake, the shedding of the old and birthing of the new, the power of protection. By changing her understanding of the dream, the dreamer is actually re-dreaming the myth.

Let's look at each type of re-dreaming to see how women are literally re-dreaming society's myths and rewriting aspects of myths that are clearly nonbeneficial.

RE-DREAMING PERSEPHONE: CHANGING THE MYTH IN THE DREAM

Jackie, a woman in my circle, has very powerful dreams full of remarkable imagery. One night Jackie's voice shook as she began to tell the following dream. It was a dream from her childhood, so she had no astrological information on it.

Persephone Dream

Jackie

I see a woman sitting in a white room in a rocking chair. She's dressed in old German- or Swiss-type clothes and she's reading from a giant book—like a big tome. She's reading me the story of my life from this book. She has very flaxen blond hair and two long thick braids. As she tells the story my point of view moves closer into her, and then I float over her shoulder toward a large grandfather clock behind her. The clock has a face that is anthropomorphic as well as being a clock face. Then the clock is telling the story as well as the woman.

The door of the clock opens, and I go into the door and into the darkness. I descend into darkness. I begin to see something colorful although I'm still surrounded by darkness. And I hear music that's like atonal organ chords and an atonal choir of voices.

Then the scene on the ground comes into focus. It's these giant tropical plants that are very saturated in color. There's a path winding its way around these plants—a dirt path. And on this dirt path are huge paw prints of some sort of animal. I descend closer, but I'm still hovering and I float over these footprints, feeling myself get closer and closer to whatever it is that made them.

I come upon a clearing. There's a little girl in the center, and she's me at three years old. She has long flaxen blond hair. She's surrounded by five bats who are dancing and singing a song that tells the story of how she is the queen of the animal kingdom and how whenever an animal dies it goes down into this world in the center of the earth. The song tells about all of the rituals that are involved with this. It's a sacred song. It's like an epic poem.

I don't remember all the details of the song, but when I woke up I remembered the tune and the words of one sentence: "And the bats were sorry when she was gone."

As the stone moved around the circle, something stirred very deeply in my body below the connection point of my dream lines—something ancient. When the dream stone hit my hand, I knew that Jackie had re-dreamed the Persephone myth.

According to the Greek myth, Persephone was the beautiful virginal daughter of Zeus and Demeter. Zeus sold his daughter to Pluto, the notorious god of the underworld, who opened the earth, kidnapped Persephone, raped her, and held her against her will in his realm. This abduction of her daughter threw Demeter into such mourning that she punished Zeus by stopping the wheat from growing. Demeter, Zeus, and Pluto negotiated a deal. Persephone is allowed to reunite with her mother for half of the year, spring and summer. Demeter lets the earth flourish during those months. But Persephone must return to her husband's realm the other half of the year. Demeter's resulting grief creates autumn and winter.

Murdock explains that "because female history has been so shattered, women are reaching back to prehistory to find elements of the woman's mythology that existed before the Greek division of power into multiple gods. As archaeologists uncover ancient cultures based on the life-giving principles of the Goddess, women reclaim the power and dignity once accorded to them, when the role of women was to protect human life and the sacredness of nature."

Charlene Spretnak's *Lost Goddesses of Early Greece* refers to the pre-Hellenic Persephone myth. According to this version, Persephone, as a young woman, found that new sprouts of wheat were especially attractive as they pushed themselves up from the earth. Persephone loved to nurture and encourage the growth of the new plants. When she spoke with her mother, Demeter, about the plants, her mother explained that their seeds are stored and fertilized in the underworld. Because she is the goddess of the harvest, Demeter remains in the upper world to draw forth the plants and feed the living. Persephone often traveled into the underworld to see the rooting, the deepening of the plants.

Persephone had the gift of vision and often saw the spirits of the dead while on her underworld journeys. She realized that the spirits often got lost in the underworld—not knowing where to go or what their new role would be. The underworld spirits were the newly dead, human and animal, who did not have the knowledge or ability to go to the land of the dead. Persephone decided to go into the underworld voluntarily and escort the spirits into their new world and initiate them into their new way of being. When Pluto heard about Persephone's acts of power in his kingdom, he became angry and called her to him. He told her that she had no authority in his kingdom. Her suggestion was that they marry. This way, she would be the queen of the underworld, thereby achieving her authority, and he would be married to the most beautiful of the celestial virgins. How could he refuse?

After the wedding, she could come and go as she pleased. Each fall and winter, Persephone voluntarily descends to the underworld to give new life to the darkness. Each spring, she ascends to the light to greet her Great Mother and share the riches of that life with the living.

This is truly a different story than the Greek telling. The Greek version of this story threw Demeter into a "manly" battle with Zeus, one that she only partially won. The pre-Hellenic version, on the other hand, gives us a win/win myth. In the older, truer version, the mother-daughter team nurtures the darkness because they know that only through transformation in the underworld does consciousness get the nourishment it needs for growth.

We all make our archetypal journeys into the underworld. We all get depressed. We all have our dark nights of the soul. Our choice is whether to go in kicking and screaming or whether to go in as an act of power. Jackie's re-dreaming of the Persephone myth reminds us all that the underworld is a place of rich color, deep connection, rooting, grounding, and profound experience. It gives us reason to return to the underworld with grace, for we know that power comes from our depths.

RE-DREAMING RAPE: CHANGING THE OUTCOME OF THE DREAM

Six dreamers, including myself, were on a retreat in the mountains and sleeping in a tipi when Freya re-dreamed rape. Freya awoke very disturbed, feeling a fear not based in her own personal history but a fear that every woman "womb-knows" regarding rape. The circle heard her dream and helped her understand that she had transformed an energy and broken an old pattern to empower us all.

Freya's Near Rape

Freya

☽ in ♐
MOON IN SAGITTARIUS

I was in a hotel like the Ambassador, meeting a friend on the mezzanine or third floor. I was returning from a trip, so I had luggage with me that I left in the lobby. When I got to my friend's room, the dining table was set with pink colors. His face was distorted around his mouth.

I left to see that my luggage was safe in the front lobby. It was being moved and I had to get it back into place. When I returned to my friend's room, there was his smaller friend who I had seen before in other dreams. My friend lifted me up into a horizontal position while his friend came toward me with a needle. He was going to stick it in my stomach. I knew they were going to rape me.

I woke up remembering how these two had mistreated other women in my dreams—had used other women as sex objects.

I decided to re-dream it. I re-dreamed that I could get out of the situation using martial arts and kicking them away from me. I returned to the lobby, got myself out intact, and returned home safely.

Freya shook with fear as she shared the dream. Erica, a very insightful seventeen-year-old dreamer, brought great clarity to the experience with her comments. She saw that these men intended more than rape. The men meant to damage Freya's dream lines by sticking the needle into her womb. Erica congratulated Freya's ability to transform the event's energy on behalf of all women.

Freya had created a healing dream for herself. Also, remember that dreams when the moon is in Sagittarius often involve physical strength, especially in the legs and thighs. Freya pulled on the energy of Sagittarius when she re-dreamed, kicking the men out of her life.

The men in Freya's dream were trying to limit her power by controlling her physical movements. Dreaming power threatens society's ability to maintain the status quo and keep control over external events. The wisdom and courage to re-dream were beautifully alive in Freya's experience. Freya no longer held victimization in her personal belief system.

This is not a simplistic or naive viewpoint. I am not saying you will not be raped if you do not dream of rape. However, we must take responsibility and accountability for our lives on every dimension. By taking the authority to re-dream abuse, rape, and victimization, we begin a cycle that disempowers those experiences in ordinary reality.

Again, quoting Deepak Chopra's Merlin: "There is nothing out there that you did not dream in here first. . . . there are infinite possibilities left. Reclaim your power; no one can dream forth a world of love and peace except you."

HEALING DREAMING
See page 45

SAGITTARIUS DREAMING
See page 23

RE-DREAMING THE WOLF: CHANGING THE UNDERSTANDING OF THE DREAM

I had not known Sharon long when she shared her dream with me.

Wolf in the Window

Sharon

I was in a two-room cabin high in the mountains. I was lying in bed with a man on my left side. He was asleep. To the right of me was a large window that looked out onto the forest. The forest was filled with tall spruce or fir trees. The ground and the trees were covered with freshly fallen snow. I was lying there experiencing the beauty of nature and the full moon reflected on the snow. Suddenly I saw a very large black wolf walking toward the cabin. He came up to the window, sat down, and looked right into my eyes. I could feel his heart and I could see a longing in his eyes. I knew that he wanted to be with me. I said to the man, "Look, there's a wolf at the window." The man jumped out of bed and grabbed a piece of wood. I said, "It's OK. The wolf doesn't want to harm us. He wants to be with us." Then I noticed that the wolf had come in the kitchen by the back door. The man raised the piece of wood to hit the wolf and I grabbed the wood from him, and he hit the wolf with his fist. The wolf cried, and I ran out the front door.

Sharon had re-dreamed Little Red Riding Hood. In the original story, Little Red Riding Hood's mother sent her into the woods to visit her poor, sick grandmother. Little Red Riding Hood was too innocent to realize the threat the wolf presented, so she told the wolf where she was going. The

poor, sickly, victimized grandmother—old women are rarely
wise in our fairy tales—let the wolf into her home, and he
ate her. If the hunter had not been nearby, the wolf would
have eaten poor Little Red Riding Hood, too. But fortunately, the man heard Little Red Riding Hood's cries for
help (although he must have been too busy to hear the grandmother's), rescued the maiden, killed the wolf, cut him open,
and miraculously saved the grandmother, too. This story presents a separated mother, maiden, and crone—none of whom
were complete.

In Sharon's dream, mother, maiden, and wise woman all
live within the same body. The dreamer/observer is simultaneously wise and connected to nature. She sees the wolf completely differently from the women in the traditional story.
Sharon understands the wolf as a call to her own nature. The
hunter is no longer an anonymous protector waiting for her
cries. He is a life partner—albeit unconscious, asleep in bed
next to her. The danger in this dream is not the wolf (*nature*)
but the fear of nature carried by the unconscious masculine.
Sharon disarms the masculine fear (*takes the stick*) and merges
her consciousness with nature (*runs out the door*). In Sharon's
dream, the feminine was liberated not by masculine bravado
but by the shift in her awareness.

Sharon's dream reminded me of the first dream Lynn
shared at dream circle. It was a recurring childhood dream.

The Heartbeat

Lynn

*I could tell the dream was coming because I heard a beat like a heart-
beat—a warning. I was in an area with sloping hills. The only thing
around was one little building like a restroom in a national park. The*

wolf was chasing me and that was the only place that I could hide. I would go into this building and go into one of the stalls and stand up on the potty so he couldn't see my feet. I would try to be really still so he couldn't find me as he circled the building.

Just as Freya had seen her rape dream as a nightmare, Lynn had always felt disturbed by this childhood dream. The dream seemed to indicate that danger was present. Yet when she received feedback from the circle, Lynn realized that the dream was full of the power of nature. The dream suggested a child's return to freedom and wildness. Lynn saw that it was her societal training which had taught her that the wolf was a symbol of danger.

Note from Lynn

I have not had a nightmare since joining dream circle. Through working with the dream teachings and listening to my sisters, my whole perception of animals, force, and darkness has changed. Fear has left me.

In some parts of Europe, the wolf is related to the Goddess. In fact, stories of women shape-shifting into she-wolves to run wild with their mates under the full moon are still told in many parts of Northern Europe. European wolf stories give us reason to believe that women first established relationships with wolves and eventually domesticated them.

The wolf is the guardian of the forest and the gatekeeper of the animal beings. The wolf and his cousin coyote are two of the most common spirit animals of the indigenous peoples of the North American continent as well as Europe.

Our folktales are stories that make nature fearful for humans and that place the spirit animals in conniving and murderous plots. Wolf got the bad end of the stick. In every story from Little Red Riding Hood to the Three Little Pigs, the wolf is bad, the wolf represents danger, and the wolf always loses. In reality, the wolf is a fiercely loyal animal who mates for life and is deeply devoted to her children and her pack.

In re-dreaming, the wolf becomes the champion of the child, the lover of the woman, and the partner of the elder. Re-dreaming calls the power of the wolf to bring us back into balance with our personal natures as well as with Nature herself. Symbology that represents nature as something dangerous and harmful to be conquered and killed no longer has a place in the dreaming. Does that mean a change is being manifested on the planet? Yes.

The Dream Weave is the earth's consciousness. It is transforming, because consciousness always changes. Our dreaming is both the mirror of the process and its co-creator. We function as potter and pot. We are actor and audience. As the earth transforms, so do we. Our stories and myths are being re-dreamed and rewritten to reflect a greater consciousness. We are the stream and the boat. The earth is the dream.

Row, row, row your boat
Gently down the stream
Merrily, merrily, merrily, merrily
Life is but a dream.

9

Re-dreaming the Masculine/Feminine Balance

After five thousand years of living in a dominator society, it is indeed difficult to imagine a different world.

RIANE T. EISLER
The Chalice and the Blade

Desire is a life-force energy that controls much of our behavior. The most sophisticated spiritual systems teach that everything we experience in the world of form is sourced in a primal and cosmic desire for balance. The energy that runs through all life and that constantly strives to achieve balance (which is called *karma* in Hindu societies) is sourced in the principle of desire.

The polarities and paradoxes of daily life represent our attempts to balance the cosmic energies. Polarities serve as a spiritual impetus to reconcile. Often, however, we are stuck in the feeling of irreconcilable separation. Separation is especially apparent in male/female partnerships. Ideally, male/female partnerships attempt to balance the divine masculine and the divine feminine. The attempts are not always successful.

Of course, we are all created from the same energy, and we all return to the same energy. But in the dimension of physical existence, we live primarily as either male or female. Our attempts to balance the masculine and feminine within ourselves and our relationships can be the richest and sometimes most painful experiences of our lives.

As dreamers, it is essential to keep masculine and feminine energies balanced. We are accountable for the imbalance our world seems to experience today, and we must work tirelessly to create a new balance.

For a few thousand years, there has been an imbalance. Masculine energy has, without question, dominated our governments, religions, and family structures. I've read every culture's creation story that I can find. Nowhere have I seen a reason for male dominance. So I ask myself this question: Why do we dream and act out a dream of violence and dominance when our purest spiritual desire is for balance and harmony?

EVETTE'S STORY

A partial answer to my question came in a story from a friend, sculptress Evette Weyers. Evette is Henoseh Hammut Anea—a Yaqui phrase meaning "woman who dances the world." She and her husband, actor Marias Weyers, are natives of South Africa. They have spent a great deal of their married lives "continent hopping." Marias will do a movie or a television show in a certain country and Evette will go with him sculpting wherever she can find clay and a table!

During one of their American stays, Evette went on a spiritual journey that sent her into the "creative void," as she called it. It is terrifying and difficult for an artist to lose the ability to create, but it happened to Evette. She joyfully described the day she suddenly burst out of her creative aridity and wrote a beautiful story. We sat in my candlelit living room by a crackling fire, and she told me the story. I felt as though she were answering my deepest questions.

This is my retelling of her story. With Evette's permission, I am presenting her story the way I heard it—as an answer to my questions:

Eve

The story opens with a beautiful goddess who walked through the hills and valleys, experiencing deep love for and appreciating the beauty of her planet. She loved the animal beings, the plant beings, the mineral beings. She loved the wind beings, the fire beings, the water beings, the earth beings. She saw the beauty of this planet as unique in all the galaxies.

She decided to call forth a human being to share this planet with her. She scooped up some clay from the earth and made a body. She called on the winds to breathe air into the body, the waters to run living liquids through it, and the fire to ignite it internally. Then she lay down to sleep and dream this being into livingness.

When she awoke, the dream was completed. There before her was a man. His delight in this planet equaled hers. His innocence and freedom were thrilling. She, being very aware of his every feeling, realized that he must not know that she was his Creatrix, lest he feel inferior and lose his ability to enjoy the miracle of life. So she spun a dream around him that protected him from the knowledge of his origination.

He suggested that they spend a day naming everything. It was a gloriously fun day of giving every sentient being on the planet its sacred name. It was a day of balance, harmony, and peace.

At the end of that day, he told her of his God and the rules of his Maleness. She was amused and wildly curious. She asked many questions. He showed her the tree from which they must not eat. She knew that she had never created such a tree, for all her beings—plant, mineral, and animal—were mutually supportive in her world. In astonishment, she agreed to go along with his rules in order to understand more fully what this partner of hers was experiencing.

Eventually, the rules got more exacting, more dominating, more ridiculous. When she decided to explain to him the truth of their existence, he called her blasphemous and shamed her. He told her never to forget that they are not the Creators but rather the created.

In her deep love for him, and in her deep desire for his life to be lived fully, she realized that she, too, had to forget their origin. Sadly, but with strong resolution, she buried the memories in her womb—so that they would be passed on in the most potent but secret ways to her offspring—and she lived the rest of her days in the shadow of the Dream.

Evette's story echoed in my heart. I saw every aspect of the story as an answer to my question regarding the imbalance between males and females. This is a re-dreaming of a myth, because it actually changes the creation story.

THE GREAT CREATRIX

The archaeological literature of the last two decades demonstrates that for a long period in our evolution, Woman was the great Creatrix. Woman was also the first gatherer, the first farmer, and the first architect—the builder of society and relationships. Evette's story reminded me that at one time, Woman knew herself as the Goddess. Evette's story places the creation myth in that ancient framework.

Why did the ancient Goddess spin a dream that allowed another way of thinking to dominate? Her passion for life? Her love? Her fierceness to protect her creations? Her determination to allow life to live itself fully? Her very womanness?

Evette's story reminded me that women are so complex and diverse, so deep and dark, so instinctive and creative, and so fully alive that they willingly sacrifice huge parts of themselves so that others might also experience aliveness. Evette's story is an allegory of the dilemma a modern woman may experience: would she rather bring pain into a relationship or betray herself? She will almost always choose to betray herself.

Evette's story represents the dreaming hidden deep in our bellies that is awakened when the dream lines and the moon connect. Evette's story represents the knowledge that must become wisdom in order to achieve balance.

After Evette shared her life-changing story with us, my dream circle began to see dreaming in a different light. Before, dreams about relationships with men had seemed mundane, psychological, and personal, even though there was always a magical quality to them. Now we understand that as each woman re-dreams her relationships with men, she re-dreams the masculine/feminine balance.

RE-DREAMING FATHERS

Carol's father had died several years before she had this dream:

Christmas Tree Named Sam

Carol

☽ in ♎

MOON IN LIBRA

MOON POWER DAY

I'm in my New York home, but it's in California or Colorado. I get a call from Barry (my oldest brother who is in New York) and he starts the conversation cryptically about an old famous football star (my father). I think he is going to say that my father is dead. I start to cry very hard, but then I realize that in waking he is already dead. I stop crying. Barry says, "He is in the hospital." I'm immediately very excited—maybe I was wrong all these years [about his being dead].

Barry says, "He's hurt and he's a tree. Enemies are trying to kill him." I have a vision of people surrounding the hospital shooting at his window. I say, "Don't we have guards around him?" I'm horrified that someone is trying to harm him.

The doorbell rings. A large, lush, dark green Christmas tree is outside my door. It's a birch.

My father has traveled cross-country disguised as a tree and is now here to escape. I see a vision of his hitchhiking as a tree—people toss him in the back of their truck, or people with station wagons put him in the back of their cars.

I know someone is watching for him. I take him into the first room, which is an enclosed porch—a room used just in the summer—where I think would be the most likely place for a tree because it has lots of light and it's cool. I want to decorate him like a Christmas tree to disguise him.

Then I decide that he will be safer in the living room. It's an internal room. I also want to see him—he came so far and I haven't seen him in so long that I want him in the main part of the house. I open the door that separates those two rooms and pick up the tree. As we cross the beautiful oak threshold, he becomes my father—younger and thinner than I remember him. He doesn't talk.

I take him into the front room. I look outside across the living room through the windows. My neighbors have built a watchtower

like a playhouse on stilts and they can see right into the living room.
They've spotted him.

Carol had this dream on her yearly moon power day, that day which occurs once a year, near your birthday, when the moon duplicates both the exact phase and zodiacal positions of your birth. Your moon power day is the most powerful dreaming day of the year.

One of the definitions of *re-dreaming* is dreaming change into a myth. Carol's dream does that. Myths about men and trees are as old as history itself. The creation stories under which most of the world lives include analogies of the relationship between man and tree. The Western myth involves the forbidden Tree of Knowledge as told in Genesis. Carol's dream addresses the myths of men and trees.

In Carol's dream we can see elements of healing dreaming. Carol's father, Sam, was the healer. He came as a birch— a tree with oils universally known to soothe pain. He came to heal Carol, and the rest of us who have ears to hear, from the pain of the conflicting belief that death is separation. Sam was dead and not dead, simultaneously. Carol's father came to comfort her and be comforted by her.

The circle commented on Sam's cleverness: a New York Jew disguising himself as a Christmas tree. However, we also realized that a Christmas tree is a tree severed from its roots. The tree no longer has the power of regeneration. In Jewish mysticism, the kabalistic tree of life is an inverted tree—the roots are in spirit and the branches are in physical existence. Sam, as a Christmas tree, points to the loss of hope in a society severed from its roots. Was this a dream story about our entire social structure's vulnerability? Are we not severed from our spiritual roots? Are we dreaming that the systems and

POWER-DAY
DREAMING
See page 68

HEALING DREAMING
See page 45

mythologies under which we have lived for so long are, like Sam, in danger and simultaneously dead because they are no longer rooted in truth?

Carol's re-dreaming restores wholeness and brings healing to all who examine the dream's meaning. Certainly, the dream addressed Carol's personal relationship with her father and her grief over his death. It also alerts us that we need to understand the transformation that our male-dominated societies are experiencing. The dream challenges us to help with our society's healing and to protect the masculine. It reminds us to root ourselves in spirit. Remember, Carol's dream does not really end; the danger is still present. If we re-dream our imbalance, the severed, endangered society will become whole.

This is only one of many dreams I have heard about ill or dying fathers. Often, women take these dreams very personally and awaken with fear. However, we have learned to examine father dreams for signs indicating that the mythology around our father system is changing.

Of course, each father dream has a personal aspect. However, father dreams also point toward a greater healing: a social healing. We are losing the "big daddy will fix it" philosophies in which we have indulged ourselves for so long. Father dreams point to the transformative, regenerative nature of the male/female relationship. We are re-dreaming the balance.

THE MALE/FEMALE RELATIONSHIP

In her book *Being in Dreaming*, Florinda Donner discusses the difference in the way men and women access knowledge. She says that men cone toward knowledge from their heads. One might picture a pyramid above a man's head as a metaphor for this concept. Men use reason, logic, and deductive or inductive thinking to arrive at a conclusion, which sits at the pyramid's point.

Women, on the other hand, access knowledge directly through the wombs. Women invert the image of the pyramid by placing the point below the navel. Knowledge vortexes into the womb through dreaming. This knowledge, however, comes from a physical expression—a gut feeling, or an intuitional relationship to knowledge. If a woman wants to understand something in her mental body, she must reframe the knowledge into words, ideas, and concepts acceptable to the intellectual community.

In our society, a fully balanced man must check his reasoning against his dreaming and intuitional experience. A fully balanced woman will check her dreaming against her reasoning side. Generally, because of personal propensities, a man's reasoning will dominate his experience, and a woman's dreaming knowledge will dominate hers. This difference explains why it is difficult for men and women to sit in dream circles together.

Because masculine and feminine relationships are so incredibly complex, books that are written on the subject are often best-sellers. The books also involve titles evoking the gods (Venus, Mars, Saturn) to help us! Truly, one of our most challenging life experiences involves reconciling the masculine/feminine balance within ourselves, our businesses, our marriages, and our parental relationships. We need help!

Sobonfu Some speaks of marriage as an "agreement of spirit." She says that when two people come together as a couple, they bring two worlds together. To open the doors between the two worlds, spirit must enter the relationship. This is what we do as dreamers: call spirit into the masculine/feminine relationship to make it whole and holy.

Unfortunately, in our present society, the split in the masculine/feminine balance shows itself most overtly in divorce. Divorce deeply injures most dreamers, and re-dreaming becomes necessary for healing to actualize.

RE-DREAMING EXES

Divorce under the best of circumstances is hard, and it usually takes years to heal. We have a generation of divorced dreaming women. I do not know the latest national statistics, but I imagine that our dream circle is not abnormal in that about 50 percent of us are divorced. The high divorce rate of our generation encourages us to begin re-dreaming male/female relationships and roles.

Many women find an ancient energy in their ex-husbands or ex-lovers that brings out all the pain of the last five thousand years. When we re-dream relationships with our exes, we also re-dream the pain patterns that our exes open, and we begin to heal.

For years after her divorce, Marilyn could not rid herself of ex-husband dreams. When she had an erotic dream, the lover turned into her ex. Even after she was happily remarried, the dreams continued. This concerned Marilyn and caused her confusion. Her psychologist had interpreted Marilyn's dreams to mean she was not fully "divorced"—she had some psychological connection with her ex. Marilyn's relationship with her ex had been highly sexual and abusive. In her deepest self, she did not feel connected any longer to her ex-husband. However, before Marilyn came to circle, she did not know how else to interpret her dreams.

After sharing her dreams in circle, Marilyn realized that she was in the process of re-dreaming the masculine imbalance in our society and that her mind was using the image of her abusive ex to symbolize that process.

In dream circle, when someone presents a sexual dream (which, by the way, is surprisingly rare), we view it as a sacred-union dream. We always tell the dreamer to "go for the ecstasy," because dreaming ecstasy evokes a body wholeness rarely available in waking reality. When all the bodies (physical, mental, emotional, spiritual, energetic, and dream) are in alignment with one another, a surge of energy moves through the person and calls her to wholeness. Sexual excitement is as close as many of us come in our ordinary lives to reaching that divine wholeness. When we are able to access it in dreaming, we pull it closer to manifestation in waking reality.

Unfortunately, society's historical dishonoring of the feminine has distorted our collective picture of sexuality. Society has blocked our memory of divine wholeness. Most women meet confusion and frustration when they peer into their ecstatic natures. Dream circle helped Marilyn see her ex as a regal consort. Marilyn's ex became the dream partner who could help her achieve the level of unity and wholeness that all humans desire. Marilyn's fear of her ex-husband's personality problems and the painful memories of the dysfunction in their human relationship began to dissolve as she honored him as her divine lover in the dream. About a year later, Marilyn ran into her ex. To her great surprise, she was able to chat casually with him. She felt no anger and walked away with a sense of closure.

Dream circle has liberated me from beliefs I used to hold about being "stuck" in my own psychology and history. Because I know myself as a dreaming woman, I feel liberated from harmful patterns. My thoughts and behavior more completely mirror my authentic self.

Like many who have divorced, Tawny suffered for years with questions of personal failure. She often shared her guilt with us about hurting her kids and ex-husband. This dream marked an amazing shift in that energy.

Deer Tracks

Tawny

☽ in ♑

MOON IN CAPRICORN

I was going to see my ex-husband to take him some things I thought he might need. His house was in the woods—a little cottage. I got there and no one seemed to be at home. The door was open. I stepped into the front room. The floor was covered with a light coat of sand. In the sand were deer prints. The deer seemed to have walked in concentric circles around the room, like an inward spiral, and then just disappeared.

Again, the man living among the trees reminds us that the trees are dreaming with us. Tawny's dream image is particularly beautiful to me. The deer tracks created a new pattern for Tawny and her ex-husband. The new pattern is the spiral—the feminine pattern, the pattern of the Milky Way, the pattern of the dream. Tawny no longer needs to worry about the pain. The men are living with the trees and the deer. They have returned to their natural selves.

Marilyn's and Tawny's dreams are only two examples of women re-dreaming ex-husbands. However, the two dreams are representative because they rely heavily on the regenerative symbols of the tree, the feminine, and sexuality. The dreams originally seemed to be highly personal, but in circle we saw a collective pattern. Evette's story helped us understand that Tawny's and Marilyn's dreams are stories resulting from the reawakened memory of our goddess origin. The dreams also remind us that the energy of the Weave is neither male nor female, but whole.

When women who are powerful dreamers break old non-beneficial patterns and re-dream new ones, they do it for everyone. Of course, Marilyn and Tawny experienced the immediate repercussions of the changes in their own lives, but now that the new patterns represented in the dreams are available, all of us have them as an option. A new potential has been dreamed; a new possibility is activated in the Weave!

RE-DREAMING FIRST LOVE

Women often come to dream circle with dreams about their first loves. The dreams are usually emotional, because most women have huge tender spots in their hearts for their first loves! After all, we only fall in love the first time once. And we never fall that innocently or deeply again.

I was sixteen when I met David. Ours was the most important relationship of my life for many years. David taught me that I was lovable. He taught me the power of love. He taught me to fall in love with life. And most importantly, David awakened the dreaming woman in me. When my magical strawberry spirits abandoned me in childhood, I closed the door on my dreamy, visionary self. However, at the hands of true love, that door was opened. I began having very powerful dreaming experiences at age sixteen.

Many years later, David and I said our final good-byes. Brokenhearted, I sobbed myself to sleep. That night was the first of my many, many David dreams.

David Dream

Connie

David came for me. I saw in his eyes that our separation was over. We were to spend the rest of our lives together. The ecstasy in my body was more powerful than any feeling I've ever known.

When I awoke and realized that this was only a dream, the disappointment was almost unbearable.

For over twenty-five years this dream, or one very similar, recurred. I was haunted by their power to make me long for a part of my past. Finally, I tearfully shared this chapter of my story with dream circle. This opened the floodgates of first-love dreams. We all cried together and mourned the loss of true love.

Then a lightning bolt of understanding jolted us. These dreams are transition dreams! When first loves come in dreamtime, they are signaling that we are in a transformation as powerful as the one we experienced when we first fell in love. We looked at other old-boyfriend dreams and the pattern was the same! First loves and old boyfriends are our dream escorts into profound transformation!

Now when David comes for me in dreamtime, I rejoice. I awaken knowing that the power of true love is active in my life, and I am "in love" again.

MANIFESTING THE BALANCE

What is it that calls the goddess out of the shadow so that her old consciousness can resurface? Her passion for life? Her love? Her fierceness in protecting her creations? Her determination to allow life to live itself fully? Her very womanness?

As each woman re-dreams her relationships with men, she re-dreams the male/female balance, and therefore she manifests the divine-masculine/divine-feminine reality. This energy is already moving in the Weave. It is inevitable. Knowingness, memory of who we are, and partnership are all to be restored on this planet. Nothing is ending—no cosmic divorce, no mysterious death, no loss of true love. All is included. Everything that we have and know integrates into the new awareness derived from the masculine/feminine balance. We remember the linear, yet we simultaneously remember only the love. The Goddess is no longer the Creatrix; the male is no longer the created. Through dreaming they have become the sacred partners of creation. This is a time of great celebration, for we are coming home to ourselves.

10

Wild Dreaming

The memory is of our absolute, undeniable, and irrevocable kinship with the wild feminine, a relationship which may have become ghostly from neglect, buried by over domestication, outlawed by the surrounding culture, or no longer understood anymore. We may have forgotten her name, we may not answer when she calls ours, but in our bones we know her, we yearn toward her; we know she belongs to us and we to her.

CLARISSA PINKOLA ESTES
Women Who Run with the Wolves

Clarissa Pinkola Estes's *Women Who Run with the Wolves* surely awakens ancient memories in every woman who reads the book. She stirs memories of our wildness, which has "become ghostly from neglect, buried by over domestication, outlawed by the surrounding culture. . . ." For many of us, dreaming is the vessel of our wildness. Only in dreaming does our wildness surface. Perhaps it's time to allow re-dreaming to bring it into our daily experiences.

WILD DREAMS

Dreaming ourselves as wild women makes us laugh. Most of us are modern women, living relatively predictable albeit highly stressful lives. When a woman brings a wild dream to circle, she is often giggly or embarrassed over the idea of her own earthiness. Judith giggled as she shared this dream:

Wild Boar

Judith

☽ in ♑

MOON IN CAPRICORN

I became a wild boar. I delighted in the earthiness of running on all fours, rutting, rolling in the dirt. I rolled onto my back. I had nipples that looked like little mouths. I couldn't remember if they were for feeding or eating.

Shape shifting and body confusion is typical in wild dreams. We can't stay within the confines of modern-day standards for a woman's body and still let our wildness express itself. Taking on the shape of a wild animal is a dreaming way to explore the aspects of ourselves that remain "over domesticated," as Clarissa would say. The wild boar with nipples that both give and receive is a perfect metaphor for the wild woman.

Jamie Sams, author of *Animal Medicine: A Guide to Claiming Your Spirit Allies*, tells us that wild-boar medicine is "the ability to confront—the courage to face challenge." Judith's wild boar most likely came to her in dreamtime to give her the courage to care for her children and herself (*nipples as mouths*) while confronting the challenges of modernity. In addition, Judith's wildness maintains the courage to do all these things without losing her contact with the earth.

Our wildness—our personal relationship with Mother Nature—is often our most powerful connection to life. Nature is our Mother, whether or not we remember her face. Lisa, a very demure and controlled business woman, shared this wild dream with a sense of amazement:

Mother Earth's Face

Lisa

☽ in ♉

MOON IN TAURUS

I was walking along a creek. I approached a bridge and saw a motor-cycle gang waiting for me on the other side. I kicked off my shoes and started running toward the bridge so I could join them. I looked down. A woman's face came up out of the earth and called my name. I was angry that no one had told me she was there. I'd completely forgotten she was there.

Lisa was at first shocked that she would gleefully run to join a motorcycle gang, even in a dream. That was wild enough. But the shock of having Mother Earth's face come out of the ground and speak her name brought tears to her eyes as she shared it in circle.

Great sadness as well as twittering laughter often accompanies wild dreams. How could we forget that Mother Nature is there? How could we walk on her face and not remember she is always calling our names? This thought is sad and brings tears to many women.

Mud Dog Beings

Paula

☽ in ♍

MOON IN VIRGO

I was leaving a meeting. I approached my red convertible, ready to get in and go for a fast ride up the coast highway. On the driver's side of the car was a big mud puddle. I couldn't get to the door. Mud dog beings popped up and asked me to come and sit with them. They were weeping and wailing. I didn't want to get dirty. I tried to get around them. I slipped and fell in. I sat and cried.

Paula felt fear from this dream. She thought it might mean that she was dirty. Women who have been sexually abused as children often feel soiled. She was terribly disappointed, because she had worked on her sexual-abuse issue in therapy for a long time. Paula thought the dream was telling her that therapy had not worked.

Wild dreams are deeper than psychological remembrances, even though the psychological aspects are certainly there. Wild dreams are reminders of our deepest origins. Mud people remind us that we are made of the earth's minerals. We are the earth. If we forget who we are, we lose our place in the universe. If we forget that we are three parts saltwater and one part mud, we lose our ability to help co-create the universe. If we forget our elemental selves, we cripple our angelic selves.

The power of self-investigation is the power of being human. You moved through the entire evolution of the species, indeed, of the universe, in the first nine months of your life. All the memory of who you are is stored in the millions of molecules that dance a unique pattern that becomes you. Dreaming is the tool you can use to recover that memory, regenerate your connection to wildness, and access your power.

POWER DAYS BRING WILD DREAMS

Fern's wild-woman dream has become one of our favorites:

Wild Woman

I was in a country school in a beautiful little valley. The gymnasium was a separate building from the rest. I was standing in the door of the gym watching a class of sixth- or seventh-grade girls, but I was simultaneously looking at the beautiful trees that were wearing all the colors of fall. I'm not sure of my role—some sort of supervisor, maybe principal.

Outside I saw an absolutely stunning wild woman riding a horse. She was about my size and age with waist-long thick blond hair blowing behind her. Her dress was deer or elk skin. Her horse was the same color as her hair, and his tail flowed behind him. She was riding very fast but with great intent, looking for something very specific. Suddenly she stopped, got off the horse, and turned into a whirlwind. She went up into the clouds, gathered power from them, and came back down as a tornado.

We quickly began getting the girls out of the gym and into a nearby ravine. Some of the girls were still in the gym when the tornado reached the door. This was an amazing tornado with unbending intent. She went in the door, not destroying the building. She didn't seem interested in hurting the people or the building. She was just gathering power.

I hustled the girls out anyway and put them safely in the ravine. Then I headed toward the main school building, knowing that this would logically be the next target of a tornado moving southwest to northeast. The first-grade class was in the front schoolyard on a nature hunt. I began taking them down to a dry creekbed.

I heard the horse's feet again. I looked west. The tornado had become a woman again. She was riding faster—searching passionately for her next target. She crossed the creekbed about half a mile to our left, then rode to the top of a small hill on the other side. She disappeared into an aspen grove.

I knew that she was going to come halfway down the hill before she got off the horse. I crossed a wooden bridge, went up the hill, and hid behind some mesquite bushes. She came down, stopped the horse in front of me, and dismounted. She turned her back to me,

Fern

☽ in ♊
♀
MOON IN GEMINI
ASPECTING VENUS
MOON POWER DAY

Wild Dreaming   151

apparently not seeing me. I leaped, encircling her body with my arms and legs. She was incredibly strong. She didn't seem to feel me, she didn't stumble, she didn't fall with the impact of my body. I had a firm grip on her.

I saw the first-grade teacher (who had seen the whole thing) run inside. I knew that she would call for help and that all I had to do was wait.

Suddenly I felt a door open in my chest. Because of the way I was holding her, our hearts were very close together. It was as if we merged. I felt the amazing power, intent, and ruthless courage of this woman. I have never had such respect for a being. I said, "I really like you." She said, "Of course you do. And I like you."

I could see a group of townspeople coming to help. They were all men. They looked like vigilantes. I devised a plan to protect this amazing creature from them without losing her for myself.

Fern's dream affected us all very deeply. The wild woman was looking for power. The power came when she and Fern became one. The woman's wildness and Fern's rational mind, when merged, became a creature more beautiful, more powerful, and more whole than any of us had ever known. The potential for wholeness is in everyone. Dreaming is our way of actualizing it.

Fern's dream came on her moon power day. Of course, moon power dreams are always important. We have consistently found that what a woman dreams on her moon power day gives her an understanding of who she is in dreaming. In other words, a moon power day is her day to be a visionary—it's a dreaming day. Her dream body is more acute, abundant, and substantive than any other day. The dream a woman has on a moon power day tells her what her role is in the collective process of "dreaming the world." Some dreaming women take

POWER-DAY
DREAMING
See page 68

all the moon power dreams of a year (thirteen moon cycles), string them together, and find an incredible story.

The moon was in Gemini during this dream. Gemini is the twin sign. Fern dreamed her sacred (wild woman) twin, and their hearts and bodies merged. Gemini dreams, you remember, are often school dreams, because Geminis love learning. In addition, Gemini dreams often show the dreamer the connectedness of all sentience. In Fern's case, nature, the wind, the "dream" school, the horse (power symbol?), and the bridge all connected into one flow of energy.

Similarly, Fern's dream came on a night when the moon aspected Venus. Venus dreams are about transformation in the emotional body. After Fern's heart merged with the wild woman, she experienced a profound change in her feelings. Fern respected the wild woman. She liked her—and she became her protector rather than her pursuer.

Also, notice the importance of the trees in this dream. In fact, all of nature—the valley, the ravine, the dry creekbed, the wild horse, the aspen grove, the mesquite tree—play a major role in Fern's dream story. Fern's dream calls the rational being to nature.

Did you know that an aspen grove is a special female symbol because all the trees of the grove grow from the roots of a single mother tree? Every aspen in a grove is a daughter of the main tree. Surely this wild woman was calling us home to the mother tree so that we may recognize our kinship.

Wild dreams are profoundly important. We re-dream ourselves and thus re-create and regenerate our wildness. Through the re-dreaming, we restore the wild woman made ghostly by neglect. We liberate ourselves from the over-domestication that has buried her. We re-dream the wild woman, and we become her.

GEMINI DREAMING
See page 20

VENUS DREAMING
See page 27

TOUCHING THE WILD WOMAN

Touching is an important symbol in wild dreams and our experiences with the wild woman. When Fern grabbed the wild woman and merged with her, she brought them both to their power.

Touching is a sacred expression in a relationship. Touch brings solidity to the dream. Touch bridges the waking and sleeping bodies. Touch honors another energy in a very intimate way. Wild dreams tell us that everything in creation has been touched in a special way and that through touch in our dreams, we will remember ourselves as women of power.

Touching is also a way of knowing. The skin is an organ of regeneration. The skin sloughs itself and then renews itself. Beautiful Painted Arrow, a Native American shaman from the Southern Ute and Picuris tribes, teaches that fingers are the rays of light extending directly from our heart. As we reach out to touch, we extend heart love into the world. As dreamers, we have been touched *by* spirit. If we then awaken and touch each other *in* the spirit of the dream, we do our worldly work impeccably.

Before Fern touched and was touched by the wild woman in her dream, the objective of the dream was to protect; the motivation, fear. After their hearts merged and Fern touched power, the objective was relationship; the motivation, love. Before touching, Fern saw with the eyes of her head; after touching, Fern saw with the eyes of her heart. The woman's touch nurtures life. Dreaming is a woman's way of touching the potentials of manifestation.

Dreaming women cannot see themselves clearly, because their nature is internal. That's why the wild woman has been so hard for us to find. As we dream in circles, however, we are finding her in ourselves and in each other. Wild woman assists us in dreaming. She gives us new dimension, new possibility, new hope, new lust for life. In that way, wild woman also helps us see the past differently. She helps us re-dream patterns that no longer serve us. Wild woman gives us the earthiness and the heart to shatter old myths and beliefs about ex-husbands and other bonds that have kept us "civilized." She leaps up out of the earth and calls our name. She becomes a tornado and gathers power for us. She speaks to us through the trees.

Wild woman has become a dreaming woman. She spins into our circles like a tornado and blows away what is no longer appropriate. Wild woman is trustworthy. She no longer runs on the treadmill of self-loathing. Wild woman's heart has opened, and she has recognized herself as power.

Note from Jeanne

Dream circle has been a profound spiritual journey. It has given me an immeasurable gift: I am no longer ashamed of being a woman. The qualities that I have kept under wraps during my adolescent and adult life are the very qualities honored in dream circle. Because of this, I feel less guarded and rigid in my daily life. My life has become more joyful as I allow my truth to be seen by others. I feel more powerful and more able to take risks.

What Jeanne says is important. She has recognized herself as power. Jeanne is not a woman who has been in therapy and learned to forgive herself for self-loathing. She is the "woman who was" before the self-loathing existed. Jeanne never hated herself. The wild-woman dream is an ancient dream—a dream of self-loving.

The wild woman is good at "dreaming the world" because she will not betray herself or her sisters. Wild woman appears out of the earth, gathers power, hurls the shattered past to the winds, and remembers who she is. Wild woman dreams the world because she is the world.

Re-dreaming the past means taking another option, experiencing history in a new way, putting one's attention on another dream line, becoming a different drop of water in the river. That's what the dreaming women in my circles are doing. Re-dreaming is not a denial of the realities of life, nor is it a naive "look on the bright side." Re-dreaming is bringing the knowing of the womb to the conscious mind. It is a celebration of the other selves that we hold in us—the "crazy" selves, the healthy selves, the wild selves, the loving selves. Re-dreaming the past is another task of the dreaming women.

PART FOUR

DREAMING THE FUTURE

Suffice it to say that a wizard's life differs from a mortal's in one very unique respect: he lives backwards in time. He is able to foretell the future because he has already lived it, and he is not crippled by memories of the past because it hasn't happened yet.

DEEPAK CHOPRA
The Return of Merlin

Dreaming the future is the real imperative of the Master Dreamer.

Most people come to the present out of the past—with energetic commitments to hold the past in place. In so doing, most people guarantee that the past will repeat itself in the future.

The Master Dreamer has recapitulated the past. She has changed her way of thinking so that it is no longer linear but cyclical. The Master Dreamer has eliminated, or at least gained control of, the veils that separate her physical body from her dreaming body. And she has used the discipline of prayer to purify her heart. In so doing, the Master Dreamer has turned time around.

The Master Dreamer comes to the present from the potential future, with full knowledge of the power of the past. She dreams the world from wisdom and love.

11

Creating the Future in Dreams

The past decides the present to the extent that the world is a machine. The future decides the present to the extent that the world is creative.

Fred Alan Wolf
Star Wave

As women, it is our sacred charge to purify and re-dream the world.... In women's teachings, first we dream the dream, then we bring the dream into manifestation, and then comes understanding.

Minisa Crumbo-Halsey,
as remembered by Connie Kaplan

A few months after my first dream circle started meeting, we noticed that we often dreamed the same symbols on the same nights. At first, I thought it was a coincidence. (When will I ever quit wasting my time believing in coincidence?) As I looked closer at the symbols, I realized that the moon was sending us a message. We were dreaming the same symbols for a reason. We were dreaming the future together!

In part three of this book, I discussed some of the ways we re-dream the past by re-dreaming our social structures. We re-dream myths and the masculine/feminine balance. We allow wild woman to be reawakened in us through dreams. All this re-dreaming lays the groundwork for releasing backward-looking, past-obsessive, addictive patterns.

Dreaming the future requires an open-minded, optimistic, and creative pattern. The symbols that my dream circle shared in common opened a pathway for more creative patterns to express themselves in dreams—and then, of course, in waking reality.

Note from Elaine

Participating in dream circle has opened a door to a previously unknown side of myself—my prophetic self. I now know I have power as a woman to effect positive changes in this world, in partnership with other dreaming women. With that realization has come a feeling of purpose and strength.

As dreamers, we stand in the present, between the past and the future. In the last few chapters we looked at how the past is being re-dreamed. Now we will examine how the dream creates the future!

INTENTIONAL DREAMING

Dreaming the future involves a profound understanding of oneself as a creator. Free will and self-determination, by definition, are a human's birthright. Learning the proper use of will and determination is one ingredient to intentional dreaming—dreaming as an act of volition.

Of course, we can't predefine a dream. We can't "order in" as if a dream were Chinese food. But we can invoke the energies that help create a dream for a specific purpose. We can ask for a dream. We can incubate a dream. We can evoke a dream.

Intentional dreaming is very sophisticated, and frankly, most people are not skilled at it. Intentional dreaming requires a paradoxical technique: using volition while surrendering personal will.

How do you do it? Through spiritual practice. When you use the four paths outlined in chapter 7, your relationship to dreaming moves out of trivial, mundane, and ordinary dream spaces. You develop skills and powers in dreamtime that enable you to practice intentional dreaming. Let's look at those four paths again:

1. If you practice the *physical path*, you will keep your body clear and you will maintain a relationship between the waking and dreaming bodies. As a result, you will be able to use waking-body intention in your dream.

2. If you practice the *emotional path*, you will eventually call back enough of your personal energy to intentionally act within the dream.

3. If you practice the *mental path*, your deeper understandings of the cyclical nature of dreamtime will give you an extra advantage as you wander in the dreamscapes. Clarity of mind is the key to intentional dreaming. Without mental clarity, you will dream chaotic and potentially misleading information.

4. If you practice the *soul path*, the path of prayer, you will place yourself in a divine space before sleep, and the dreams will enforce the truth of that space. If you go to sleep in faith, you will experience grace during the dreamtime. Your dreams will direct you toward the beauty way—the path most beneficial to you.

Intentional dreaming involves volition *and* surrender. To completely control a dream would be folly. You may as well stay awake! Intentional dreaming is a little like surfing. You act, but first you surrender to the wave and allow it to carry you.

There is also a "why" and a "why not" to intentional dreaming.

The "why" is that intentional dreaming becomes a path of service for you. When dreaming truly becomes a spiritual path, you use dreamtime constructively. You maintain consciousness, even while in the dream. This is not lucid dreaming—a dream in which you realize you are dreaming. An intentional dream could be any of the thirteen types. An intentional dream is a dream in which you are consciously interfacing with Great Dreamer to achieve an outcome. That outcome, however, is not defined by you alone.

The "why not" involves our limitations. We are human. We are capable of vast expanses of consciousness—but even at our vastest, we do not have the whole picture. It is dangerous to think that we know how anything "should" be. Intentional dreaming must include a deep humility—a "not my will but Thine" attitude—and a profound appreciation for the gift of life. It must involve a respect for the unknown in dreaming.

Intentional dreaming is powerful. Intentional dreaming creates the future. Of course, some other dream types also participate in creating our future. But when we practice intentional dreaming, we involve ourselves in bringing forth the beauty way for all beings. Even when we ask for dreams for ourselves or our family members, we are affecting a greater circle than our limited perspective can see and know.

Intentional dreaming is masterful dreaming. It demands respect, and it brings great rewards.

NOTE FROM KAREN

I have always had dreams that were prophetic, but I have discounted them, either because I didn't want to see what they presented or because I didn't trust my own psyche. Through dream circle, I have become more aware that dreaming is my work, prophecy is my gift. I no longer separate myself from my dreaming.

FEAR OF CREATING THE FUTURE IN DREAMS

Many dreamers are afraid of dreams of the future. They are afraid to ask for dreams. Intentional dreaming frightens many people because they feel responsible for the outcome. Some people don't want to be accountable for the future. Some people prefer to pretend that they have nothing to do with the future. However, thinking we have nothing to do with the future is like not thinking about death so it won't come. Or it is like not looking at the gas meter in your car in hopes that you won't run out of gas.

We do create the future. We create the future by dreaming. That is what dreaming is—moving into the realm of possibility and giving life energy to potential manifestation.

Whether we have telepathic or clairvoyant dreams and get immediate feedback from them or whether we never see our dreams "come true," we still dream the future.

The next few chapters describe some of the images and story lines that our circles have dreamed. They are dreams of a future that is changing, beneficial, and hopeful. They are dreams that will put your minds at rest. We are dreaming the future together, and it is a good future.

12

Dream Vehicles as Symbols of the Future

The soul is a winged charioteer, whose wings fall away in coming to earth to be born in a terrestrial body.

THE WOMAN'S DICTIONARY OF
SYMBOLS AND SACRED OBJECTS

One night at dream circle we discovered that since our last meeting most of us had dreamed of driving. The dreams were either of a car going the wrong direction on a one-way street or of a car going against the flow of traffic. Something changed in dream circle that night. We examined the symbols we were dreaming collectively. We realized that calling our similar dreams a coincidence was irresponsible and inappropriate. The power of working in a spiritual community like dream circle requires that we do not ignore when spirit speaks to us simultaneously. We entered a new level of dream work that night.

In the car dreams, we immediately saw several consistencies:

1. The car was a vehicle for consciousness.
2. If we were driving our own cars, we were breaking the rules: going the wrong way down one-way streets, going against the flow of traffic, or finding ways around laws.
3. If others were driving the cars, there was a life-threatening danger: people were shooting at us, accidents were imminent, or there were car thefts and kidnappings.
4. Women were taking charge of the vehicles.
5. The vehicle was changing form.

VEHICLE FOR CONSCIOUSNESS

Many of us had dreams indicating that the car symbolizes a vehicle for consciousness. Lynn's dream gave us a positive view of the expanding consciousness we all seemed to be experiencing in the car dreams.

Driving West

Lynn

☽ in ♒

♆

MOON IN AQUARIUS
ASPECTING NEPTUNE

We—a black man, a small boy seven or eight years old, my mom, Chad, and someone else—were in a car and I was driving. We were driving to the beach to catch the sunset. The sun was on the left, and it was huge and orange. It was ethereal driving through the clouds on the road. Some cars were stopped on the freeway. Everyone was going the same direction as if they were making an exodus. We had made no plans—we had just started going, as if we were pulled there. When we got there, we walked and went through doors into a glass room. I went through a different door. There was sand on the floor. There were lots of people sitting in the sand to watch the sunset.

In this dream, Lynn was driving her own car, indicating that she was in integrity with herself. The setting sun's beautiful colors were calling Lynn, her passengers, and the other dream characters to attention. The sun lured them to the potentials of light—the movement west toward the transformation of consciousness.

Just before dawn that morning, the moon aspected Neptune. Neptune dreams are often collective and give us an image of the moving collective consciousness. It is worth noting that Lynn's Neptune dream brought her to the sea (Neptune's turf) on the west side of our continent.

NEPTUNE DREAMING
See page 29

In many traditional cosmologies, west is the direction of death and rebirth—transformation. Orange is the color of the flame of truth that resides in the heart of all sentient beings. The glass (or sometimes crystal) room represents a prayer place—the temple of the soul.

The imagery in Lynn's dream reminded me of the Chariot card in the "Motherpeace" tarot deck. In *Motherpeace: A Way to the Goddess through Myth, Art and Tarot*, Vicki Noble describes the driver of the chariot as "Neith, who some scholars think is the oldest Goddess in the world . . . and represents the intellectual light of the mind." My dream circle saw Lynn as the Goddess, steering her vehicle toward the light. We saw Lynn moving her vehicle "westward" in consciousness in order to merge more completely with the transformational energy that creates the future we dream together. Lynn and her passengers had no plans and no needs. They just surrendered to the call of transformation, as did the other dream characters, and they joyfully followed that call.

Futuristic dreams move humanity toward actualizing potential that evolves and enlightens consciousness. Futuristic dreaming gives us hope for our children and our past (our parents). This kind of dreaming redefines the present in terms of the future.

Note from Elaine

Dream circle is a gift that has had a tremendous effect on my life. My vehicle, my body, is no longer my prisoner but now my regal carriage. Connie has shown me how to bridge my dream state and waking state through the heart. She has taught me to love humanity, embrace life, and commit to help better this world and walk in harmony with humankind.

BREAKING THE RULES

While discussing our futuristic vehicle dreams in circle, we discovered many dreams in which women drove the vehicles and broke all the driving rules. One dream in particular was curious:

Sunset—One Way—East

Laura

☽ in ♑

MOON IN CAPRICORN

I was following Kevin in his car. We were going somewhere heading south on Laurel Canyon. I made a right-hand turn onto Sunset Boulevard (west) and realized it had been changed to a one-way street going east. I pulled up to a gas station right next to a cop who looked at me. I explained that I didn't know they had made it a one-way street. He handed me a ticket and asked me to write my name on it. I talked to him a while. He then relented and didn't write me up. I told him thank you, thank you, thank you. Then I went off again. Kev was waiting in his car.

Interesting. Sunset Boulevard is a wonderful, winding street that stretches from Union Station in downtown Los Angeles through the cities of Hollywood, West Hollywood, Beverly Hills, Westwood, Brentwood, and Pacific Palisades, ending gloriously on a descent toward the ocean with a view to beyond the beyond. The beauty of Sunset Boulevard is in the westward drive toward the sunset. Why would it have become one way eastbound?

Laura was able to negotiate the awkwardness of the situation with grace. She didn't question or intimidate the officer—the keeper of the law. Laura simply communicated with the officer and succeeded in winning his support.

Laura's dream clarified the car dreaming for me. The symbolism of the car is more than an update of the chariot—the vehicle of consciousness. The car symbolizes movement toward the inevitable. The car is the dreamer's karmic vehicle moving toward balance. The Goddess is returning to her rightful place as driver of the vehicle.

Social rules are no longer in alignment with the Weave. The "rules," in fact, don't exist in the Weave at all. As Fritjof Capra points out in the chapter entitled "Patterns of Change" in *The Tao of Physics*, "All phenomena in the world are nothing but the illusory manifestation of the mind and have no reality on their own."

Why indeed would Sunset Boulevard be one way eastbound? Because the roads we are traveling socially and collectively are just that: going the wrong way. Dreams of driving the wrong way or driving against traffic are actually dreams of going the right way in a network of wrong rules. The keepers of the rules (symbolized by Laura's cop) know on some level what the drivers are doing: waiting for the impetus to set the rules right. As we dream the future, we must dream the rules that allow for the proper and beneficial flow of energy.

Futuristic dreaming assists social change. The dreaming pattern is the chart of potential manifestation. It is the Weave of the Great Dreamer who knows all possibility—who contains past, present, and future within every breath. Nothing of the physical world can touch dreaming, for dreaming is beyond the physical. The physical can only point us toward an evolutionary understanding of the world.

First comes the dreaming, then the change, then the understanding. This means that elements of change come in dreaming. The next step involves activating that change. Only after the manifestation are we able to fully understand the message of the dream. We dream the future, and then we manifest the future in the present.

WOMEN'S TEACHINGS
See pages 4 and 161

The car dreams we discussed in circle were telling us to reevaluate the directions we were taking in our lives. The dreams were calling for a change. The dream car is the vehicle that takes us through the journey of change. In the dreams discussed in this chapter, the dream car is the vehicle that assists us in breaking old patterns. The fact that so many dreamers had the same experience during the same time period indicates that the change is magnifying—the time has come.

Amazingly, I spoke with women all over the country that week about our car dreams. Other women were having them, too. What's interesting is that everyone felt fearful about the dreams—out of control. When we came together collectively, however, and found that we were all breaking the rules, the fear melted into curiosity and excitement. Discovering that you are not alone—indeed, that you are connected in profound and mysterious ways to other beings—liberates you, lifts your load, and gives you permission to be the visionary.

DANGEROUS DRIVERS

In dream circle, we looked back over the year and saw that before the spurt of car dreams occurred, we had many dreams in which we were not drivers. Almost without exception, the dreams where we were not the drivers were of danger, fear, and disaster. In my dream, anger also entered the picture.

Daddy Is Driving

My family was going to a family reunion. Daddy was driving. He kept falling asleep. I didn't want him to drive anymore. I was going to offer. Mother seemed hell-bent determined that he would drive. I was furious.

Connie

☽ in ♌
MOON IN LEO

My dream indicates that there is danger when the historical father-centered system drives the dreamer's vehicle. The unconscious father was in control, and the equally unconscious mother was blindly supporting the dangerous pattern. The dream could, of course, represent the psychological dynamic within the dreamer's family. In fact, it probably does. However, it would be irresponsible to view the dream with personal glasses when the other circle members have similar car dreams.

The next dream points toward the same energy—the daughters in the backseat seem to have a keener awareness than the father who is driving.

Pay Attention

I was with my parents going to one of their friend's house. It was up a winding road. My father was driving wildly. I told him that this was a one-way street. Just then a car came down from the wrong direction. I said, well it's supposed to be. People don't pay attention.

Laura

☽ in ♓
MOON IN PISCES

Still another dream takes us to a similar realization:

Stuck in the Mud

Mary

☽ in ♓
MOON IN PISCES

I dream I'm riding in a red Volkswagen Bug. Vance is driving. John is in the front passenger seat. Terry, Mitch, and I are in the back. Vance gets mad at me for giving him directions although he clearly doesn't know where he's going. . . . He's heading in the wrong direction. Vance drives past a demolished building site on the edge of the city and starts down a dirt road into a desolate terrain. The road ends in a big red mud puddle. The car plunges into the mud and starts to sink. I jump out the window, but no one else gets out. They all disappear, along with the car, into the mud.

The dreams Laura and Mary had point out that when someone else is driving, the trip and vehicle are in danger. The dreams, again, if considered from a personal point of view—as psychological dreaming would suggest—call the dreamer to evaluate her life and specifically whether she is allowing someone else control over her life's direction. However, when viewed in light of the collective, the dreamer can see the dreams from a teaching perspective. The dreamer is being reminded of what she already knows—the feminine principle requires that the dreamer drive her own vehicle.

GODDESS TAKES CHARGE

An encouraging aspect of the car symbols was the discovery that, in many cases, women are taking charge of the vehicles. The dreams discussed earlier were dreams of other people in control of the vehicles. Represented below we have another set of car dreams in which women are driving their own vehicles. The women know where they are going, and they are prepared to take responsibility and control.

I'm Driving

Laura

☽ in ♉

MOON IN TAURUS

We were all in my Honda. I was driving. We went around some very sharp curves on a narrow road. I had to slow down to nothing just to make it. It was hard; the car felt heavy. They may have all been afraid, but I knew it would be OK unless someone behind me got too close.

Don't Lose Control

Lynn

☽ in ♒

MOON IN AQUARIUS

As I continued to follow these people, I was speeding to catch up and cross the highway. Three cars coming from the opposite direction turned right in front of me so close I was amazed we didn't collide. I was speeding down the road on the other side of the highway now and felt my car going out of control and skidding to the left. I thought I must slow down so I don't lose control.

These two dreams indicate that the act of taking control requires slowing down—to carefully measure all the elements in the journey into consciousness. These dreams also exemplify, like many other dreams in circle, the caution women exhibit when they begin a new dreaming process. Clearly, for many thousands of years, women have not been in the driver's seat in social vehicles: government, education, medicine, and science. At this time, however, we are slipping into the driver's seat in more and more arenas, and it all starts in the dream. We are taking control in a woman's way—slowly, gently, cautiously, and with all our feelers out measuring consequences at all times.

FREYA'S JAGUAR

My friend Freya had the name of one of my favorite goddesses: Freyja, the Scandinavian Queen Mother. When I think of Freyja, I conjure up a regal image of her driving a chariot pulled by the powerful midnight black cats through the battlefields, forests, and villages. Truly, Freyja reminds me of the great goddess guiding consciousness into life—bringing the future to the present.

The dream Freya shared at dream circle one night almost brought tears to my eyes as I realized she was indeed dreaming the great goddess back into control of the vehicle. Freya died suddenly and unexpectedly just as I completed this book. I will always remember her as I pictured her with my dream eyes while she read this dream:

Small Room on a Hill

Freya

☽ in ♓

♃

MOON IN PISCES
ASPECTING JUPITER

I was on top of a hill in a small room where I was to tell my worst secret. It was going to be very hard to do. The color of sweet baby blue permeated the dream. There was a rainstorm and water was leaking in the corner of the back porch.

Suddenly I was driving my big antique Jaguar in traffic in New York City to kill time.

In the first part of the dream, Freya was the High Priestess. In tarot, the High Priestess sits on a hill in a throne that resembles a small room. She has pillars on either side of her symbolizing the polarities—black and white, past and future, male and female. She is sitting in the present holding the scroll containing the Akashic records (*everyone's worst secrets*). The fabric behind her and the fabric of her dress are both blue, and they merge to become the waters of the stream of life.

Suddenly the High Priestess (Freya), the most sacred of elders, finds herself steering her antique Jaguar through the streets of New York City, certainly as formidable and regal as Freyja and her cat-drawn chariot. The most interesting words of the dream were "to kill time." To kill time is to create timelessness.

Freya's dream of the divine goddess taking control of the vehicle is also a dream of delivering human consciousness from the narrowness of linear time to eternal timelessness— the feminine cyclical time. Freyja has returned through dreaming to escort us into a new dimension.

The moon aspected Jupiter, the good-fortune planet, the night of Freya's dream. Remember, Jupiter dreams often bring information about shattering old systems to allow the new. The image of Freya's telling her "worst secret" would represent shattering—a hard thing to do. But shattering catapulted Freya into the driver's seat and took her out of the passive position.

JUPITER DREAMING
See page 28

Freya was not alone. Many other women have dreamed themselves into mystical animals in the form of cars. These dreams are shamanic in nature because of the shape shifting in the dream. The "medicine" brought back from the dream is indeed very healing to the circle.

We Had a Purpose in Common

Laura

☽ in ≈

MOON IN AQUARIUS

I was going somewhere, sitting in the front passenger seat of a car, a beautiful old Jaguar. Then it became a bus full of college students. Somehow I did a little flip and my body lurched out of the top of the bus, but I was flexible and I bounced back into the seat unharmed....

In the bus I felt camaraderie with the people and identified with the common cause. We were all close. Someone was massaging my feet. I felt content with all those people. We had a purpose in common.

In this dream, Laura was not the driver, but she was experiencing the power animal as the vehicle. The Aquarius nature of the dream accounts for the sense of camaraderie. In this dream, Laura brings forth the Aquarian Age, the age of great brotherhood.

In the next dream, the symbol is the horse. Lynn is driving, taking control, and using the power of the symbol to direct herself safely into the future.

Blue Mustang

Lynn

☽ in ♑

MOON IN CAPRICORN

I got into an old blue Mustang and was driving really fast trying to catch up to everyone. Most of us had separate cars, but some drivers had two people in their car. I was racing to catch up. On the other side of the highway, up a distant hill where we were headed, I noticed a pattern of pillars and old buildings that looked like ancient ruins. There was a winding trail up the hill. The pattern was visible from a distance. The trail led up to an ancient temple that looked like the Taj Mahal, and I thought how great it was that we were going there. I also thought we were really going there—it didn't seem like a dream.

The jaguar is the sacred and mystical animal of the southern part of our continent. Jaguar—the Mexican magical cat—is surely the cat that would pull an American chariot like Freyja's. Jaguar often appears in dreams of the women of this continent.

The mustang is a common symbol that bridges the European and American Dream Weave. The Europeans brought the horse to the North American continent, and the horse dramatically changed the lives of the Native Americans. Now the mustang is being dreamed as a blue vehicle, the color of the High Priestess, and the car is steered by feminine energy. I once heard Heather Valencia refer to a blue-car dream as a blue-endorphin dream—a dream indicating the transformation of a physical body into the essence of goddess energy.

Consciousness is moving into a new position—a new relationship to balance. When consciousness shifts, balance seems to shift. Dreaming is telling us that consciousness is shifting toward the feminine. I find this to be encouraging.

NOTE FROM JEANNE

Seven months ago I lost my job. When I told Connie, she shared a dream she had a few weeks earlier that was precognitive about my work experience, although at the time she didn't know it. As a result, I have decided to change careers. I plan to study healing arts to satisfy my need to nurture others. I have come to see the dreamtime as energy that precedes waking consciousness and waking reality. As dreaming women, we dream a new reality. I regard this work to be the most important work I do.

THE VEHICLE CHANGES FORM

Dreaming is also foretelling a change in the form of the car. Our society is changing, our species is changing, and our personalities are changing. The future is presenting itself to us. We see our future's change symbolized in dreams about a new type of car. The following dream represents our changing future. I was driving a new kind of service vehicle—an electric bus.

The Electric Bus

Connie

☽ in ♊

♄

MOON IN GEMINI
ASPECTING SATURN

I had a very interesting electric car. It was shaped something like a small bus. I had enough power to travel six hours. I picked up two homeless men—one black, one white—in New York City. The black one had iron hands like garden tools. I bought them both big sandwiches and something to drink. Then they fell asleep. I kept driving until my car needed to be recharged. The men were completely transformed. I let them out and told them I'd come back every week so that at least once a week they could eat well and have worry-free sleep.

GEMINI DREAMING
See page 20

The electric-bus dream is a combination of re-dreaming the masculine/feminine balance and changing the vehicle. The dream came to me when the moon was in Gemini, the place of my natal moon. Gemini dreams, you remember, are often twin or mirroring dreams. The black man and the white man enter the vehicle as polarities and mirrors (the "history" and "future" represented by Freya's High Priestess's pillars) and are transformed by surrendering to the direction of the feminine energy. Yet the vehicle of the feminine, the car, which represents the human personality-carrying consciousness, does not pollute the air and requires rest and time to recharge itself. The electric bus is a more "human" vehicle, if you will.

The moon aspected Saturn the night I had this dream. Saturn dreams often carry information about restriction, limitation, and walls. In the electric-bus dream, the men felt the protection and nurturance of the feminine futuristic vehicle. The security of that limitation restored the men. The promise that the vehicle would return cyclically gave them a future of hope.

In this next dream, Beth was looking for her daughter, Hannah. She had seen clues around the house indicating that someone had come in and taken her daughter. Beth took the situation into her own hands.

SATURN DREAMING
See page 28

My Grandmother's Opal

Beth

☽ in ♒
♂
MOON IN AQUARIUS
ASPECTING MARS

My daughter was lost. I wanted to drive through the neighborhood and go to the police station. My uncle and his family showed up in the driveway. They suggested that I take their car, which turned out to be my grandmother's Opal. It had a sidecar, like an extra passenger seat. I got in and started to drive, but the brakes were faulty, so I switched cars.

Opal—the stone—has connections with the Goddess Ops, the pre-Roman Earth Mother, whose annual festivals were called Opalia. The name of this stone may also have come from the Sanskrit *upala*, "valuable stone" (*The Woman's Dictionary of Symbols and Sacred Objects*). Because the opal unites the sacred colors of white, green, red, yellow, and blue, it is the Philosopher's Stone in some schools of alchemy. Considering these historic connections, the opal is truly a transformational vehicle. Interestingly, the moon aspected Mars during this dream. Mars dreams often involve minerals. This time the stone was a vehicle!

Beth, in waking reality, had learned to drive in the Opal inherited from her grandmother. In this dream, her grand-mother's vehicle developed a sidecar—the car enlarged itself for the transportation of more energy. Mars dreams also often involve the use of energy—the expression of personal will or volition. The fact that the car had no brakes is a warning. We must carefully dream the vehicle of change so that it will be appropriate to our needs! In some cases, we must create new vehicles, such as the electric car in the previous dream, rather than drive a "redecorated" used model. This is an example of a situation where it is inappropriate to rely primarily on the past to determine the future. As dreamers, one of our tasks is to know when to leave that which no longer serves us and to move on.

Along that same line, other dreams depict a vehicle with the potential to change form. This dreaming reinforces the need to have one's energy available at every moment. One can fully embrace the present if and only if she has her energy available so she can be ready to adjust to the needs of the moment.

The dreamer—the vehicle, if you will—who has fear about objects changing form might experience fear in a dream where her vehicle actually shifts itself. In this next dream, I was driving a transformational vehicle.

My Car/The Boat

Connie

☽ in ♉

MOON IN TAURUS

I was driving home going north on the Pacific Coast Highway behind a slow car. There was an ocean storm. The driver in the car in front of me was driving badly. The car stopped. I went to see what was wrong. The car was a hull—no seats, no seat belt for the baby, who was rolling around in the back. They were afraid to go on—afraid the undertow of the overlapping waves would wash them into the electric wires. I discreetly turned my car into a boat and suggested we take it out beyond the waves. I hoped they wouldn't notice anything extraordinary.

Changing vehicles—the electric bus, the Opal, and the car/boat—are shamanic dream vehicles. They shape-shift to transform energy in the most benevolent and appropriate way. Shamanic dreams take the dreamer into states of consciousness that allow her to return with healing for others. The dreamers of changing-vehicle dreams were working for someone else: Beth was working to find her daughter, I to serve the homeless men and save the baby in the car in front of me. The dream vehicle helped the dreamers create a better future for others!

SHAMANIC DREAMING
See page 49

In tarot, the Chariot represents the astrological sign of Cancer, the crab. Crabs carry their homes on their backs wherever they go. That is a heavy burden—yet they are "at home" wherever they go. Cancers are always prepared to serve. Cancers' dreaming chambers are always present. Cancers are ever ready to bring forth the future.

In dreaming, the car holds the same set of symbols in modern society as the chariot did in ancient civilizations. The car is the vehicle of the present looking toward the future. According to our dreams, a twenty-first-century set of tarot cards would depict the car as the vehicle of consciousness that adapts to the needs of the moment based on the potentiality being dreamed by its driver. The shamanic car is the vehicle of the Master Dreamer who looks toward the present from the future.

The car is the vehicle that carries us into relationship with other vibrations. We are moving toward purity as represented by Lynn's dream: going to the purifying waters of the ocean. We are moving toward new relative placement in the dreams of driving the wrong way, driving against the flow. We are moving toward awareness when the vehicle changes form to fit the moment. We are moving toward innocence as the Goddess takes control of the vehicle again.

We are the vehicle that carries consciousness to its destiny. The future is the vehicle that holds all potential. Dreaming is the vehicle that delivers the future to the present.

13

Dreaming Water

Not only the thirsty seek the water;
the water as well seeks the thirsty.
                                    RUMI

ater dreams are prolific in our circle. We feel that
the water is indeed seeking us—quenching our thirst
for consciousness. In this chapter, I want to discuss
only two aspects of water dreaming: the clarity of the water
and communication with water beings. These two themes
show up frequently in our water dreams. We are dreaming the
future through the appearance of these two images.

THE CRYSTAL-CLEAR WATER

Time and again, as women share dreams of oceans, lakes,
rivers, and rain, one phrase repeats itself: "The water was
crystal clear."

This repetition of the phrase sent me to research books.
My question was: Since at this time we are not experiencing

crystal-clear waters on the planet, what is dreaming saying? In fact, according to the environmentalists, we are killing the planet with the intensity of our pollution. How can the dreaming women see crystal-clear waters in a time of immense oil spills and wanton sewage dumping? I realized we must move more deeply into the clear-water metaphor.

The psychologists of our time who work with dreams call water the symbol of the collective unconscious. I considered the possibility that water dreams are reminding us that the collective unconscious is clear, but this interpretation did not really fit. Psychologists write mountains on the dark and murky nature of the unconscious. In fact, by definition, the *unconscious* cannot be clear, can it?

Faces in the River

Connie

☽ in ♎

♃

MOON IN LIBRA
ASPECTING JUPITER

NEW MOON

I was in a place that was half building and half canyon. I was on level five or six of the building side. I heard a powerful sound. I looked to the canyon side. A huge tree had fallen and was rolling down the canyon toward a river at the bottom. I saw that several people were going to be killed by the log. I ran to try to help, but by the time I got to the river, it was too late.

I looked into the crystal-clear waters as the river flowed by me. I saw the faces of the dead people floating by. It was not frightening or gruesome. In fact, their faces had turned into ceremonial masks and their lips were moving.

I put my own face very close to the surface of the water. They told me things about consciousness, and they simultaneously probed my brain for information. There was an exchange of information between me and the water.

In this teaching dream, water was not the unconscious at all. The water was more conscious than I. Water was communicating to me and taking information from me that I couldn't even hand over consciously. I had no idea what the water was taking from my brain; I just knew that it was telling/showing me that death is an aspect of consciousness and that the communication process, through the waters, was powerful and *crystal clear.*

In prepatriarchal times, water represented ultimate consciousness. Water marks the site of most goddess shrines: springs, wells, lakes, waterfalls, and the sea. The Creatrix and water are one. In the language of ancient Sumeria, water was AMA, that which comes before MAMA. In fact, the "M" of "MAMA" is an ideogram for the waves on the waters, according to Barbara Walker's *The Woman's Encyclopedia of Myths and Secrets.*

Out of the woman's waters all things are born. MAMA. Water is the unique consciousness and life-sustaining force of our planet. Through crystal-clear water, we experience ourselves as self-aware beings. Water is not the unconscious experience of our hidden selves. Water is the conscious experience of life.

Some say that the revised modern symbolic meaning of water uses the word *unconscious* because when the feminine principle sustained continued attack, it naturally submerged deeply into the crystal-clear waters of consciousness. This image is similar to Evette's story about how the Goddess, out of love for her partner, chose to bury her memory of creation in her womb—in her water/birthing place. In the womb, the memories were held in sacred trust and passed on genetically to all generations.

And now, at this time, dreaming is reawakening the memories of water's original meaning.

TEACHING DREAMING
See page 43

EVE
See page 133

Wedding at the Beach

Jeanne

☽ in ♈

MOON IN ARIES

I was at a wedding celebration at the beach. The water was crystal clear and I couldn't stop looking at it. I was amazed.

Incredible Water

Laura

☽ in ♐

♃

MOON IN
SAGITTARIUS

ASPECTING JUPITER

Went driving. There was a sandy beach. I met friends there. As I turned the corner, it was the most beautiful water in the world. It was crystal clear—aqua blue-green with waves crashing down in the same color. It was awe-striking. There were different people there. I video-taped everything. There was some kind of kachina display or sand painting set up. Many different things. I can't remember everything, but the water was incredible.

These are two samples of water dreams shared in circle. The clarity and beauty of the water is so magnetic that the dreamers cannot even pay attention to the other details of the dream. The message of this dreaming seems to be that consciousness is clear and attractive. Consciousness longs to see itself and know itself. When we encounter that longing on the Dream Weave of truth, it symbolizes itself as crystal-clear water. The clarity and beauty of the water reminds us to see each other with clarity.

WATER AND INNOCENCE

My daughter, Sara, was eight when she had this dream:

I Earned My Wings

Sara

I was in my room. An eagle flew in the window. He signaled for me to get on his back. I did and he flew back outside.

He took me to two mountains with a little narrow valley between them. At one end was a waterfall, and a little creek flowed through the valley. The water was so crystal clear that it looked like diamonds were in the bottom of the creek.

We landed and I saw that we were in a village, only you couldn't really see it from the air because the houses were built into the side of the mountain. The sun came up behind the village, and in the afternoon the sun warmed the houses.

Before the eagle left, he told me I'd just gotten my wings. I began to try to learn how to fly. It was fun. A woman who looked like my mom, but was an Indian, came out to encourage me to fly higher. Then another woman who looked like my mom and had lighter-colored skin came and started telling me to come down because flying was too dangerous.

I looked down. The woman who told me to come down seemed more like other people's moms or a teacher. The Indian seemed like my real mom. So I just kept flying and watching how the water curved around the houses.

This dream is the beginning of Sara's teaching dreaming. The dream calls our attention to a very important aspect of dreaming. In dreamtime we are able to shatter the physical laws in order to gain experiences and perspectives not ordinarily available to us. Sara, guided by the crystal-clear waters and encouraged by her Indian mother, learned how to fly. More importantly, Sara learned to be conscious of the "real mother"— she learned to discern what is worth hearing. I can only hope that Sara is representative of the new little dreaming women who are being born now. I can only hope the crystal-clear waters are flowing through every little girl's dreams in this powerful way.

Sara's vision of clear water points toward an understanding of how light and water interrelate. The mere fact that Sara dreamed

TEACHING DREAMING
See page 43

water as diamonds tells us that she "womb-knew" that consciousness and light are inseparable. When we drink water, we drink consciousness, we drink light. When we bathe, we purify ourselves in liquid light. When we swim, we float in light—we fly.

Sara's sweet dream, delivered to us from the innocence of a child, is so sophisticated that it piques our attention. On the personal level, Sara's dream gives her permission to "fly." On the collective level, it gives a dreaming sister her wings and welcomes her into the lodge of dreamers. On the highest level, it points directly to two aspects of consciousness required of all dreaming women: innocence and purity. Water and light awaken the dreamer to her "real mother" and her right to fly. We all knew that Sara had dreamed the future. She will always see her present from knowing her future.

Consciousness is calling dreamers home. Whether we are sitting in circles together or not, consciousness calls us into the future.

Note from Elaine

At the end of the day as I fall into bed, I pray that I will be able to turn off the tapes of everyday life, go to the other side, and return to Source. Joining dream circle has shown me how to go to the other side and return with power. The power can change my life for the better and help me embrace life, love humanity, and commit to the tremendous amount of work necessary to put my life in balance with Mother Earth.

WATER-MAMMAL DREAMING

A second aspect of water dreaming that is consistent and frequent is communication between dreamers and water mammals.

Whale Bite

Laura

☽ in ♏

MOON IN SCORPIO

I dreamed of whales, many swimming and jumping. I was standing on the side of the water, on the edge, but sort of in it. One whale jumped up at me and sort of bit me, but not really. She just opened up the fleshy place between my thumb and forefingers and gave me some things—information perhaps.

The day after this dream, one of the whales at Sea World had an accident and died. It was the mother of Baby Shamu. The platform that Laura was standing on in her dream was similar to the platform around the arena at Sea World. Laura's dream is an example of clairvoyant dreaming.

In water dreams, communication seems to exist primarily with mammals. Certainly other kinds of sea creatures show up in our dreams, but they don't actually communicate with us. Shark dreams, for example, seem to be about physical "knowing" rather than interspecies communication. I had a particularly curious shark dream on a moon power day.

Legs and Butt Dream

Connie

☽ in ♊

MOON IN GEMINI

MOON POWER DAY

I was swimming in deep ocean water. I saw someone's butt and legs sticking out of the mouth of a shark. I swam closer to see who it was. To my astonishment, it was I. Suddenly the perspective changed. I was looking into the shark's belly. One side (camera right) was red and set up like a bar. Camera left was a dark cave. Lindsay sat at the bar in a slinky, sequined red dress. "Are we in the belly of the whale?" she asked. I said, "No, it's a shark, and sharks can't digest people, so everyone just stay calm and he'll throw us up in a minute." Carol was in the dark cave looking mischievous. I was acutely aware that I must not move or the shark would bite down.

TEACHING DREAMING
See page 43

This teaching dream tells me that nonmammals have a different sort of dreaming relationship with us—they can't digest us. Dreams with sharks and other sea creatures are more primal. They are about eating and being eaten. These dreams are about assimilation into a different, ancient vibration.

Many dreams about mammals are "kinder, gentler" dreams. The mammal dreams shared with me in dream circle are so numerous that I can only include a few:

Eight Dolphins

Laura

☽ in ♌
MOON IN LEO

At the sea in a tent. Talking on the phone to a friend. Saw eight dolphins in front of the tent in an arc. I was very excited. One came closer and closer. I leaned forward out of the tent as it approached me. It came right up smiling. I petted it for a while. I was so elated. I was telling my friend everything as it was happening. Then the tent spilled forward and some of my stuff got spilled into the water. It was very clear and still water, so it was easy to retrieve my items.

Look, Whales!

Jeanne

☽ void

I was at a river's edge, the Columbia, with my sister and mother. I saw whale spouts very close to the shore. One, then two or more. I exclaimed, "Look, whales!" and ran to the water and was waving as a wave broke. To my left was a small gray whale about fifteen feet long. I exclaimed in happiness again, but my sister and mother couldn't see them. A beluga whale came up to me and I stroked its tail. The gray whale came up to us. Then a sea lion came to me and I petted its head and neck.

Jeanne's dream above reminded me of a dream I had a few months earlier:

Can't You See?

Jeanne

☽ in ♐

♃

MOON IN SAGITTARIUS
ASPECTING JUPITER

I was at the Santa Monica pier with my two children. We walked on the pier for a while. Then we went to the sand. As we began spreading our towels and making our space, I saw several killer whales playfully leaping just about twenty feet off the shore. I pointed and exclaimed and began talking to the whales, telling them I'd come out with them as soon as we got settled. The children couldn't see them. I even took my daughter's head in my hands and pointed her eyes in the right direction. She still couldn't see. I just could not believe that they couldn't see.

The similarity of these three dreams attracted my attention. The whales were only visible to, and apparently only communicating with, the dreamers themselves. The other people in the dream could not see them.

As I ponder these dreams, I am caught in a frustrating bind. My years of work with dreaming tell me that one need not interpret or analyze dreams in the traditional sense to understand their meaning. One dreams the dream, acts on it, and then understands the dream. Yet I want to know what the whales have for us, and I don't know how to get the information any way other than through a mental interpretation. I can't go and live with the whales and wait for understanding to come. I believe that the mammals are speaking to us in dreaming, and our comparatively tiny brains just are not able to decode the messages. I find this frustrating.

NO PATTERN

I must also make a confession here. In all my dream work, I have found astrological charting to be valuable, helpful, and a source of illumination. However, this is not so in water-mammal dreaming. I can't find a pattern of any sort—that is, not for me, personally. I dream water mammals in all signs and all configurations. Other women in dream circle may have found some patterns. For example, I know that women who have a natal moon or natal sun in a water sign find that their most potent water-mammal messages come when the moon is in a traditional water sign.

I think the key lies in the mind—human mind versus cetacean mind. Whales and dolphins have brains much larger and more sophisticated than ours. So what do they do with all that gray matter?

A few years ago, I had an occasion to swim with a small group of dolphins. At the time, I knew very little about dolphins, except that their brains are much more sophisticated than ours and that their infant death rate is practically nonexistent. I was astonished when I got into the water. I don't like swimming, although I'm good at it. As I eased into the water, I dreaded the cold, alien sensation. Suddenly I found myself surrounded by consciousness—not water. I was inundated with an expansive, peaceful, playful, and heartful feeling. A dolphin swam directly up to me and—I swear I'm not lying—put her head on my shoulder. I threw my arms around her neck and began crying like a child who had been lost in a shopping mall and finally found her mother.

The whole experience was emotional and joyful. I did not stop crying all day. Fortunately, my family is used to a mom who sobs over the beauty of anything, from a pretty leaf to a well-produced "reach out and touch someone" telephone commercial, so they just let me cry and went on with their vacation.

Since then I have talked with lots of people who also have swum with dolphins or have been close to whales. They all have the same experience: a feeling of profound peace, a sense of an open heart, and a playful joy. How do the whales and dolphins do that?

DO WHALES DREAM?

I still don't know all I want to know about whales in waking reality, but we are all becoming quite familiar with them in dreaming: perhaps it is because we live so close to a whale-migration passageway, but our circle dreams about whales almost weekly!

Orange Whale People

Jeanne

☽ void

I was walking along a beautiful coastal highway, maybe in Northern California or Oregon. I saw someone herding a pod of orange whales along the lane of new blacktop highway. They were going toward the ocean. They were supposedly a rare type of orca—no dorsal fin, more like twelve-foot manatees, with bright orange topsides. I think they were white and black on the bottom. I was very excited to see them. They were moving south and were just at the end of their journey, because a cove was nearby.

After my experience with the dolphins, I did some cetacean research. We have evidence that whales are our ancient, ancient ancestors. The whales may have even come out of the sea, lived on land (*walked the blacktop*), and then even-

DRIVING WEST
See page 168

tually returned to the sea at one point in history. I wonder why? Does it have something to do with the size and sophistication of their brains? What is the bright orange topside telling the dreamer? Is this the same "orange" message that appeared in Lynn's dream of driving to the beach and watching the orange sunset?

One fact I learned from my research particularly struck me: the increased brain size in whales and dolphins is the area of the brain that performs computation. In other words, their capacity to remember past events and hold a perspective on possible future events increases with their brain size. In addition, I learned that the parts of a dolphin's brain that determine body control and neurological development are the same size as ours. That's very exciting. What dolphins have that we don't have is a larger capacity to understand the present in terms of the past and future. Does that mean they hold more knowledge of the potentials that exist on the Dream Weave than we do? Does that mean they access a wider computation of beingness?

Jeanne is our circle's most prolific whale dreamer. She always wonders: What do whales and dolphins do with all that information? They aren't architects building futuristic cities, they aren't scientists reaching into space, they aren't housewives going to the market and driving carpool. What are they doing?

I think whales and dolphins are dreaming. I think they are speaking to us in dreams because they are dreaming with us. I think they know that dreaming is a collective process, an interspecies process, a global process, and a galactic process. I think they are dreaming with us, dreaming with the trees, and dreaming with every ounce of sentience on the planet. I don't know if we will ever understand dreaming together, but I think we can learn to understand that we are dreaming together.

I give thanks for the water dreaming. I know that our blissful experiences with the crystal-clear water and our amazing contact with water mammals accesses a new dream line. I cannot say it any more beautifully than Jeanne does in her dream:

Star Dolphin

Jeanne

☽ in ♏

MOON IN SCORPIO

It's nighttime, and my friend and I are on a very high and very long pier that extends miles over the ocean. The pier is very crowded with people. We're aware that they're starting to queue up for something. I start to go toward the back of the line but realize that we're right where they're beginning to queue up, so we take our places in front. It's windy and very starry. As we look up I see a three-dimensional transparent dolphin in the sky. She is outlined by points of light. We see that she has a baby dolphin inside of her. She comes from the stars and hovers about two feet above our heads. I walk up to her and take her tail in my left hand and say, "Thank you very much. You teach us so much."

14

Dreams of Death and Destiny

". . . my death is sitting with me right here."

He extended his left arm and moved his fingers as if he were actually petting something.

. . ."Think of your death, now," don Juan said suddenly. "It is at arm's length. It may tap you any moment, so really you have no time for crappy thoughts and moods."

DON JUAN, as quoted by Carlos Castaneda
Journey to Ixtlan

If we fear future dreaming and intentional dreaming, then surely our dreams of death are feared the most. Even women who have been in dream circle for years will often recoil from hearing dreams that involve death—their own or others.

As dreamers, however, it is important that we deeply understand the many aspects of death dreams. They may be prophetic, but not usually. Prophetic dreams are typically

PROPHETIC DREAMING
See page 41

highly symbolic. One would not usually dream of a "death"; one would typically dream of an unusual growth or an atypical experience with an animal ally if one were prophesying biological death.

Death dreams are destiny dreams. They prophesy a transformation. Death dreams bring us knowledge and information about our soul's contract with life. They make us remember we are alive. As don Juan, Carlos Castaneda's teacher, said to him, "You're alive because death hasn't taken you. Be glad! In that way, death is your best friend."

One of our primary fears is the fear of death. Ironically, death is our only guarantee. The only thing you know for sure is that you are going to die. Interestingly, when you fully realize this, the feeling is quite freeing. Liberating yourself from fear of death liberates you from fear of the future. You are free to dream a future of life and hope!

Women have been dreaming about death forever and always. The fear surrounding death dreams comes from the isolation that one experiences from the dreams. If we have a dream circle with whom to share the dreams, we usually discover that we are not dreaming alone and that, in fact, we have picked up a strand on the Weave that is quite collective. Remember that I mentioned in chapter 9 the many women who reported dreams of their father's deaths. Only when the women realized the collective nature of their dreams was their fear released.

GRANDMA'S DREAMS OF DEATH

My husband's grandmother admitted to being ninety-five the last time I saw her. Everyone knew she had been misrepresenting her age for years. I wondered how old she must be if she admits to ninety-five. One hundred and twenty?

During that particular visit, Grandma talked to me about her history of death dreaming. She would only speak of the dreams in a whisper:

"I dreamed I saw my cousin carrying two dead babies on her shoulders. The next day I found out she had died unexpectedly that night.

"Oy, I must be the devil.

"I was sick in the hospital. I dreamed I was stepping into the grave and my father came, pushed me aside, and jumped in instead. I woke up, called the nurse, and told her I had a nightmare. She comforted me. They did not tell me until six weeks later that my father had died the night I had that dream.

"Oy, do you think I'm the devil?"

Grandma was serious. She believed that she was evil because she had the gift of dreaming. I tried to comfort her. I tried to exorcise her mind of her fears. I tried to explain telepathic dreaming. In both of Grandma's dreams, the people in the dreams were already dead (by only hours) when she had the dream, so we would call these dreams telepathic rather than prophetic. Grandma amazingly dreamed the information that relatives were on their death journey.

I tried to tell her what an incredible dreaming woman she was. I tried to tell her that there was nothing devilish or evil about her talent. Grandma was a skilled dreamer and an amazing psychic. It was her belief system that made her "the devil," not her dreaming. I tried and tried to tell her this, but she didn't seem to hear me. Grandma was too afraid. She told me she had never told anyone else about those dreams. She had carried the secret for eighty years—or a hundred, depending on her real age. Before I left, she said, "It's all right if you should write about me in your book." I smiled, hoping that meant she had ingested at least a little of my message.

TELEPATHIC DREAMING
See page 40

In the way that every dreaming woman *knows*, Grandma Kaplan *knew* that she was not the devil. She *knew* that there was something deep, profound, and important about her dreaming. Grandma *knew* that her dreams must be shared. I was happy to oblige.

A few months later, Grandma Kaplan died, quite peacefully. The night of her death, she passed her dreaming legacy on to her granddaughter, Susan. That night, Susan dreamed that she was sitting on the front porch of one of her old houses watching her daughter and cousin's daughters at play (all Grandma's great-granddaughters—but none of the great-grandsons—were in the dream). Suddenly, Susan heard a car horn. She looked up to see Grandma and Lois (Vic's mother, who is dead) driving by in an old Buick convertible. They were waving happily and saying, "We'll see you later." Susan awoke the next morning to a phone call informing her of Grandma's death. That is telepathic dreaming at its best.

Grandma gained an understanding and wisdom regarding her death dreaming in the last few months of her life and, in fact, gave her death dreams as a birthright/death gift to her granddaughter and her great-granddaughters on the night of her death.

DREAMING THE DEATH CEREMONY

Dreaming about death gives us the gift of our destiny. Destiny calls us to the future.

Black Pearl

I dreamed that I went into initiation with a healer. He dug a shallow grave and had me lie in it. He stood at my feet on the right side.

I was apprehensive, but as he began the ritual, I merged with his vision and was embraced by his power. I saw with his eyes that I had eight black shadowy spots on my body, below my right rib. We began to work on one spot. It was hatred. The hatred was vile.

At first I went immediately to my mother with it, thinking it was a hatred I had for her, but as it started to dissolve I saw it was a hatred of the way women had become, behaved, and been treated. I felt that it hadn't been safe for women, that it was survival.

As I began to feel this compassion, the blackness dissolved and there was a pearl. When the pearl was illuminated, I could see that there were stones in the other seven black areas in my body, but the only other one that came through was amethyst, though I don't know for what reason because the dream ended.

Katy

☽ void
♂
MOON VOID
ASPECTING MARS

The black-pearl dream came when the moon aspected Mars. Mars dreams are often physical-body dreams. They tell us about memories we have stored in our bodies. Interestingly, Mars dreams are also often mineral-kingdom dreams. Katy found stones in her body—memories that could have caused illness (*shadowy spots*) and possibly death, but when the spots were fully understood and filled with compassion, they became jewels. This death dream became a healing dream for Katy.

MARS DREAMING
See page 27

Many years ago, in waking reality, I underwent a ceremony in which I dug my own grave. Then, under the loving, watchful eye of a medicine person, I spent the night in the grave. Many cultures all over the world have similar ceremonies in their initiations. I was astonished at the sensations I experienced that night. I expected to be terrified, cold, lonely, and sleepless. To my great surprise, the earth held me as if I were her baby. The earth was warm. I slept and dreamed. I felt at peace, at home, silent. Not a day goes by that I don't remember that sweet, sweet night. I dreamed of death, and death was anything but fearful.

I wonder if "fear of death" is a myth that is being rewritten like Little Red Riding Hood and Persephone. I wonder if "fear of life" is a more accurate description of what keeps us paralyzed—fear of power, fear of self-actualizing, fear of being who we are. The dreaming tells me that death gives us the gift that allows us to meet destiny.

Death dreaming pushes a woman into the future. Death dreams deliver a dreamer to her destiny. Fear is actually eliminated when death dreaming is shared in circle, because death dreaming points to a transformational consciousness that asks the dreamer to live life more fully. The dreamer will fall more in love with life every day!

WOLF IN THE WINDOW
See page 127

PERSEPHONE DREAM
See page 121

DEATH'S IRONY

Irwin was an extraordinarily talented musician I knew while I lived in Tennessee as a young woman. When I was spending time with Irwin, I always thought, "This must be what it was like to hang out with Mozart." Irwin's talent was so all-encompassing that it drove him crazy. He once told me that he couldn't remember ever having had a moment, waking or sleeping, when music was not in his head. As a result, Irwin used drugs and alcohol in an attempt to quiet his mind. It didn't work. Instead, the drugs and alcohol opened other parts of his mind—the funny parts.

Irwin was one of the funniest men I had ever met. I can remember many times when I would literally grab my cheeks and beg him to quit making me laugh so that my face could relax from the smile cramps! Everyone who knew Irwin knew about his humor and borderline insanity. Once, I was doing a show in Nashville with Lucille Ball, and I introduced her to Irwin. Irwin made Lucy laugh so hard she had to stop rehearsal. That is a funny man.

I awoke from the following dream about Irwin with vague curiosity, because as much as I loved him, as much time as I had spent with him, and as long as I had known him (nineteen years), I had never dreamed about him.

Tickle Torture

Connie

☽ in ♐

MOON IN SAGITTARIUS

I was traveling with a group of people on a bus. I believe we were a chamber orchestra on a tour in the desert. The view from my bus window was beautiful.

Irwin was the bus driver. He would get on the bus last and partition off the front so that none of us could see him. It made me uncomfortable because I didn't know what he might be doing up there. I was concerned for him. Also, I wanted to see out of the front of the bus.

We had lunch at a diner. I talked the other guys in the orchestra into kidnapping Irwin and tickle-torturing him until he agreed not to partition the front of the bus. Everyone was excited. "Yes! Tickle-torture Irwin. How many times has he tickle-tortured us?"

One guy said, "Wait. What if he won't agree?"

I responded with exaggerated humor, "Then this is tickle to the death!"

Three weeks later, my sister called to tell me that Irwin had died. Because my prophetic dreaming often occurs three weeks before the event, I knew that this one-time-only dream of Irwin had something to do with his death. I asked her to find out the details and call me back. My sister Nancy was having the after-funeral gathering at her house the next day, so she said she could find everything out at that time. That night, I went to sleep thinking about Irwin and had a second dream:

Irwin Fellini

Connie

☽ in ♎

MOON IN LIBRA

FULL MOON

MOON POWER DAY

Nancy came and told me that Irwin had made a videotape just before he died. She didn't have the courage to see it alone. Would I look at it with her? We put it in the machine. It was a very funny home movie that Irwin had apparently written, directed, produced, and starred in. He was an outrageously bizarre Fellini-esque character. I wondered if his death had also been bizarre?

Nancy called back the next day to tell me the circumstances of Irwin's death. His friends had told her that he had been particularly depressed in the last few weeks before his death. Irwin was spending a lot of time alone, and they were actually worried about his frame of mind. For his birthday, April Fools Day, Irwin's friends decided to throw a big party to cheer him up. The party lasted three days, as musicians' parties sometimes do. On the last day, they had made a videotape. Then, later, they went to the video-rental store and picked out some Laurel-and-Hardy movies to watch. While watching the movies, Irwin started laughing and apparently had a heart attack and died.

Imagine my shock as I tried to comprehend the information. Irwin had died laughing. He had been "kidnapped" by his musician friends and "tickle-tortured" to the death. I slowly, so slowly, contemplated these facts. Dream circle pointed out to me that somehow, three weeks prior, I had picked up Irwin's destiny—his date with death—on the Dream

Weave. My love and concern for Irwin created a vibration in dreaming that allowed me and his friends to re-weave his death without interfering with his destiny. We made it possible for Irwin to die laughing in the presence of loved ones rather than die a more lonely, more tragic death behind his partition of depression. Irwin died the ultimate ironic death.

Dreaming is not just personal. Dreaming is collective. We dream dreams for each other. We dream the world into being. If we forget this, we forget who we are.

A DATE WITH DEATH

I met the incomparable Malidoma Some many years ago before he and Sobonfu were married. Someone called and said, "There's an African shaman in town, and you simply must get a reading." I am a sucker for intrigue and new experiences, so I was on my way before I could really think.

It was a rainy day in Los Angeles. That means the water was pouring from the skies in opaque sheets. Rain in Los Angeles also means that everyone in the city abandons traffic rules, and a decision to drive is one of life and death. That shows how much I wanted to meet this guy. I decided to drive. As I slowly meandered around the hills of Hollywood looking for the address, I was feeling slightly uncomfortable about the instructions I had received on the phone: "Go around to the side gate and into the backyard. There's a Doberman, but he is usually friendly. Go back to the guest house. Malidoma will be waiting for you."

"How smart is this?" I thought. "I need a sign." Just as I pulled up in the front of the house, the rain stopped. There was my sign. I was out the door and face-to-face with that Doberman in a second.

I walked into the guest house and saw an impish black man sitting in the middle of a completely vacant and totally white room. He wore the traditional garb of his West African Dagara tribe. His face broke into a wide smile and he said, "What are you doing with a white face?" I laughed and knew I had met a relative.

STRAWBERRY SPIRITS
See page xvii

In our first meeting, Malidoma reminded me of the strawberry spirits. I swear, I had never told anyone about the spirits. I had even convinced myself that I had made them up. How could he see my strawberry spirits in a ragged little divination cloth filled with shells, stones, bones, and seeds? I don't know, but he did.

From that day forward, Malidoma Some has been a source of great spiritual strength and profound insight for me. After Sobonfu joined him in America, our families became "village" and we have spent many years enjoying each other's company.

Prior to this dream, however, I did not know that I was a source of spiritual help for him:

Malidoma in White

Connie

☽ void

♇

MOON VOID
ASPECTING PLUTO

Malidoma had done a seminar on Saturday night. He was not feeling well, and it was a little unorganized. He was supposed to talk to a Sunday-school group the next morning. I took him to the church where we were to spend the night.

He was burning with a fever when we got there. We sat on a couch. He put his head on my chest near my heart as if listening to my heart helped him deal with his disease. I put my right arm around him, my left hand on his head. I told him I'd help him. I said, "I'll hold you until this is over."

Morning came and we were still in that position. His fever was very high. People started peeking in the door to see if he was ready to speak. I went into the next room to change my clothes. I had lots of trouble finding matching stockings.

I went back into the room and found Malidoma sitting on the couch in a white outfit—similar to the traditional one he usually wears, but all white. He was still burning hot and seemed to be disappearing. His body wasn't very substantial. I told the church people that he would not be speaking and went back to put my arms around him.

Eventually, Sobonfu came and took him away in a beige 1960 Imperial. They didn't say good-bye, but I saw them leave.

I did not have any ideas about this dream when I awoke. I jotted it down and sent it to Malidoma and Sobonfu. The next week he called and told me that the dream was more important than I could understand. When the letter came in the mail, Sobonfu was just leaving for the airport to join Malidoma in a nearby city. He had been away for a week or so, and while he was gone, he felt as if he were under some kind of psychic attack. He was physically ill and felt that he may be dying. Sobonfu was rushing to join him.

Sobonfu read my letter on the plane and was deeply moved, for white is the color in which the Dagara people dress their dead. She realized that I had sensed the extreme circumstances of Malidoma's present condition in my dream. Malidoma and Sobonfu believe that when I was "holding him until this is all over" in my dream, destiny somehow shifted for Malidoma and allowed him to live longer.

For me, it was not surprising that I would sense such important life-and-death information when the moon was void and aspecting Pluto. When the moon is void, I often have very important "message" dreams. Pluto dreams, of course,

VOID-OF-COURSE
DREAMING
See page 24

PLUTO DREAMING
See page 30

are often indicative of an underworld journey. I apparently perceived that Malidoma was on such a journey and needed a traveling partner!

One month later, I had a second dream in which Malidoma and Sobonfu arrived at a reception in a helicopter, like dignitaries. They stood in the receiving line while famous people such as Bob Hope and Johnny Carson filed by to pay respects. When I reported the dream to Malidoma, a sigh of relief came from him. He and Sobonfu had performed a ritual and asked the village elders for intervention on his behalf. They had been waiting for dreaming to tell them that danger had passed. My dream brought the news they needed to reassure them that Malidoma's "date with death" had been postponed. Apparently, Malidoma has a larger destiny to meet at a later time!

DEATH AND DESTINY

My experiences with Irwin and Malidoma gave the dream circle insight into the powerful partnership between dreaming and death. In both cases, if I had known the worldly circumstances of the men in my dreams, I probably would have done something differently—something a little more desperate that would interfere with destiny—and ruined the beauty and power of the experiences. As it was, I did not change destiny. Instead, I discovered a vibration on the Dream Weave and offered myself as a conduit for making the vibration manifest appropriately and beautifully. I believe it is also what Grandma Kaplan did in her death dreams. I believe it is what dreaming women do all the time, whether or not they are aware of it.

Death is the aspect of the dream that drives us forward to our destiny. Destiny is the aspect of the dream that is the future. Destiny holds the potentials for us personally, for the collective, and for the mother/father being called consciousness. Destiny and death are partners, not to be feared but to be lived. Truly, dreaming with death tells us that we are to live the dream.

PART FIVE

LIVING THE DREAM

15

Giving the Gift

*Mind flowing along the superstructure of intention, as expressed in crystal forms,
precipitates the form, the pattern of one's life. In this way we are all relatives in the
dream of life.*

> DHYANI YWAHOO
> *Voices of Our Ancestors*

The dreamer's job is to dream the dream and give the gift. Giving the gift means bringing the energy of the dream to life by embodying the energy so that it may be manifested. In other words, giving the gift means living the dream.

Writing about dreaming is difficult because it is hard to put something that cannot be said into words. Dreaming is an energetic experience more than a verbal or physical one.

To know dreaming is to know the true self. To know dreaming is to realize that we are not who we think we are. To know dreaming is to know that form is metaphor. We can't verbalize this knowing. We can only imply it with the right combination of words.

Great Dreamer is the metaphor I have used in this book to express the source of truth on which the universe hinges. It is a term too big and all-inclusive to be really understood. Great Dreamer is a term that is almost too sacred to name, because it points toward a concept too vast for comprehension. The term is like God, Elohim, or Wakan Tanka. Great Dreamer is that which Is, the I am that I am. Through our dreaming and living, Great Dreamer moves into form.

One way to look at dreaming reality versus waking reality is to take note of our body positions while we engage in each type of activity. Most of us prefer to sleep and dream on the horizontal plane, and when we are awake, we prefer to be dreaming on the vertical plane. Waking and sleeping are two perspectives of energies we bring into form as dreamers on behalf of Great Dreamer.

A dreaming woman knows first and foremost that she is being dreamed. She knows that she sits on the Dream Weave, the grid of consciousness, according to the way she can best serve and nurture the whole pattern. A dreaming woman is a woman of faith who rests in a state of grace. Her work is to give life to the energies that Great Dreamer wants to see. A dreaming woman's challenge is to surrender to the work so that her ego and personal will do not deter her. Dreaming is sacred work.

We are much more than who we think we are. We are multiple realities and vibrations crystallizing simultaneously into form. As all realities come together in certain combinations, we attain new awarenesses.

We are metaphor. We are an aggregation of meanings that taken together mean something else entirely. When we surrender to the fact that we are being dreamed, and when we know that we don't exist in the limited ways we think we do, then we gain insight.

Melissa, one of the women in my circle, spent her whole life walking a thin line between waking dreaming and sleeping dreaming. She had trouble determining one from the other. Because there is no real support system in our society for dreamers, Melissa also felt that she was walking a thin line between sanity and insanity. When she first came to dream circle, she came with the hope and expectation that we would help her draw a more substantial line between her realities.

One of the reasons Melissa often mistook the two realities for each other was that she dreams more auditorily than visually. Each of us has senses that are more acute and more developed than the others. Dreaming uses our most highly developed selves to get important messages through. Melissa hears with extraordinary acuity. When dreaming has a message for her, it tends to come in words with no images attached.

Melissa joined us at a dream-circle weekend during which we did some very intensive work toward understanding ourselves as dreamers. One afternoon, while everyone else hiked and rode horses into the hills, she decided to nap in a tipi. She had a teaching dream that was also an oracular dream:

ORACULAR DREAMING
See page 46

Life as a Dream

Melissa

)) void

I was told to look at my life as dream, to analyze it as I would a dream. Everything is important. How would I interpret where I put up my tent if I described this weekend as a dream? What are the messages that I am constantly getting? Day-to-day life offers the same information about my path as does the dream. I need to take the same integrity into my dreams and into my life. If I am true to the way I want to be, it doesn't matter if it is real or a dream. There is no difference between the two states. This whole experience is about learning and growing. If I hold my own, I work twice as fast (or more). Everything matters, no matter what state it is in. My experience is what is important, not the realm from which the experience comes.

I cried with delight when Melissa shared this in dream circle. Melissa's dream gave her the help she needed to draw lines between her waking and sleeping realities. In addition, her dream gave each of us a profound teaching about the nature of dreaming.

The job of a dreaming woman is to hold with integrity and impeccability a dream-thread that weaves through all experiences, waking or sleeping. Then she is *living the dreaming* and giving the gift. She opts for a life that gives her access to, and relationship to, all things. The dreaming woman is in love with life and fully accepts the fact that life is in love with her. When the dreaming woman allows herself to dream and share the gift, she gains insight. That is what dreaming is all about.

It is also important to note that Melissa's dream came when the moon was void of course. Our dream circle gets its most powerful dreaming information when the moon is void of course. This is especially true of my pattern, but I also find it to permeate the whole circle. When the moon is moving through the specific energy of a sign on the zodiac, our dreams carry a different charge. However, when the moon moves into a nonspecific aspect, even for a few hours, the information is directive if the dreamer is simultaneously able to receive. As dreamers, I encourage everyone to be particularly alert to any messages received at void-of-course times of the month.

During the dream weekend mentioned before, each woman went out alone and performed a very specific personal

VOID-OF-COURSE
DREAMING
See page 24

ceremony with stones. The stones represented the lines of light around the womb—the dream lines. Each woman built a circle of stones around herself and then crawled into the self-created womb for her ceremony.

Melissa had a beautiful experience during the ceremony:

Bead on a Necklace

Melissa

☽ void

I now turn to the east-southeast. My view is across the valley, over the cows, up the tree-covered hillside to the blue sky. As I stare at the sky, I relax. The experiences in the previous directions were emotional, but I feel calmer now. Suddenly a line from infinity comes from the sky, over the mountains, through the trees, across the road, and up the hill to me. I can see it, though it has no color. A bird is crying. A hawk soars by. I feel this line come into my womb and up into my heart. I can almost see it as it comes through me. It moves up to my throat, and more tears come. The line goes up my head and out again. I watch as it extends into the sky and over the hills out of my sight, leaving its presence behind as it continues on. This line has no end. I am hooked into its pattern like a bead on a necklace.

Is that my role? A small part in a large pattern, a pattern that needs me to continue the energy (necklace)? If my string breaks, the necklace cannot connect. With me it continues its endless loop. A dream within a dream? This vision of a line and beads is like a dream.

I don't feel as if I have any choice in this. The line goes through me, and it always has, and for this lifetime that's the way it is. I do have a choice of how I deal with the information. I can use it, or I can fight it, but it is here to stay. I can't break the necklace; I can only put a kink in it that will stop the energy flow and be very uncomfortable.

And that is the way it is. As dreamers, we are connected. We have a choice whether to hold the dreaming in integrity or create a kink. We are the gems with which Great Dreamer adorns herself. Our job is to keep all the facets of the gem polished and beautiful so that we will dream a dream of beauty for our children. That is what we do for each other in dream circle—polish our facets.

A New Stone

Katy

☽ void

NEW MOON

SOLAR ECLIPSE

I dreamed I lived deep in the mountains in a simple way. I had been removed from people and civilization for many years. It was a long and difficult path to get where I lived.

One day the earth shook violently. When the shaking stopped, I went out to see what had happened. I could see that the earth had split into a deep crevice and that I was now further separated from the world. I could see people suspended on a broken-ended bridge on the other side of the chasm. There were fires behind them. I knew some people were going to jump into the crevice. I knew people would someday come to the side I was on and that I must prepare a place for them.

I looked into the earth and saw that she had opened up to give us a new stone that looked like a combination of opals, topaz, and turquoise. These stones were important to this new way of life. I gathered them like food. I saw them growing up from the crevice and showered onto the land. As I walked home gathering the precious gems, two tigers came and walked by my side.

VOID-OF-COURSE
DREAMING
See page 24

Katy's dream came while the moon was void of course and on a night preceding a solar eclipse and a new moon. It was a big dream.

This dream tells us what dreaming women do. We live "separated from people and civilization" in the sense that our relationship to the ordinary world comes more from the blend of many dimensions of reality than from a single reality of everyday life. If we believe that we dream alone, we are alone. But the tigers, the sacred animal of ancient dreamers, were no surprise to Katy. The dreamer is never alone as long as she is in integrity with the dream.

The images of the earth's giving us stones and of our becoming dreaming beads, as Melissa became on her "necklace," are two that touch me very deeply. The mineral kingdom is the bone structure of the earth's body. Our dreaming tells us that the earth is revealing new aspects of herself to us—she is giving us a new structure, a new skeletal support, and a new consciousness. In turn, we adorn the earth as jewels on the cosmic necklace.

Everything we know in form comes from the principles of the universe woven in truth on the Dream Weave. This is the lesson I began to learn when, as a child, I met the strawberry spirits. Discerning truth has been my life's work ever since.

The mineral kingdom represents the oldest and most experienced, if you will, aspect of "form" on the planet. The "new gems" are gifts from the old order of life. The stones are dreaming gifts that open "new dream lines" extending from very ancient sources.

The beads on Melissa's necklace are assisting us in new understandings of where we sit on the Dream Weave. They remind us that although we may be only a small part of a large energetic pattern, we are necessary for the continuity of the pattern.

We pass the dream stone in circle to remind ourselves that we are small parts of a larger pattern. We allow the stone to rest in our hands and exchange a vibration with us. We awaken

⊚

FACES IN THE RIVER
See page 186

the stone, and the stone awakens us. Just as the water and the dreamer exchanged information in my dream of water consciousness, the stone and the dreamer exchange information in dream circle.

Like other collective symbols that we dream, I cannot begin to represent all the mineral dreams I have ever heard in one chapter, but I do want to invite other dreamers to regard their mineral dreams as dreams of connection with others.

Everything felt magical the night Elaine read to the circle this exquisite dream of a desert made of ancient crystals. The magic might have come from the quality of her voice, or it might have stirred in the candlelight, or it might have been that no one seemed to be breathing.

Crystalline Desert

Elaine

☽ in ♐

MOON IN SAGITTARIUS

I'm in a white crystalline desert. Dunes. I've been underground in an excavation site. Two others keep floating in and out. I can see the strata. I say, "How fragile this all is?" I wonder if it has the strength to support everything on the surface. I ask them how long they usually stay here, since the dust and the winds were picking up. They were staying longer. I remarked that it would be easier to find one's way out of a major city than to be lost here.

When my circle heard this dream, we all felt transported to a dreaming planet. The whiteness of the crystalline dunes, the fragility of the excavations underneath, and the ferocity of the winds awakened all of us to an inexpressible knowing in our wombs. Just listening to Elaine's dream with dreaming ears palpably changed the vibration in the room. Suddenly, for a few moments, we were all beings of light. We had insight.

Elaine's dream transported us to a space of integrity that weaves through our lives and our dreams. The space was clear, cleaned by the winds, striated by the ages, vast by definition. We were in the land of all possibility. The "others" remained faceless and nameless, because in the dream space, we are of one heart, one body, and one mind. There is no "other"; there is only the circle. The others were staying longer because the work was incomplete.

Elaine's dream speaks directly to the work we are doing in circle. Many of us live in large cities, because large cities need us most. "It would be easier to find one's way out of a major city than to be lost here" speaks to the belief we have that we are alone and lost. Yes, to be lost in the dream would be lost beyond description, but it is impossible. The crystalline dunes of Elaine's dreamscape interconnect with the Dream Weave as well as with major cities, rain forests, deserts, ice caps, and mountains. Every form in every dimension is connected to the Source.

We may feel lost, but we are not. We may fear getting lost, but we can't. My sister Nancy and I were living in the same house, both talking to the nature spirits, and feeling lost and alone. But we were not. Dreaming doesn't lose the dreamer.

Every woman longs to know herself through the eyes of her sisters, just as surely as Great Dreamer longs to see herself through her dreamers. Our relationship with one another is what gives us the gift. We long to work in circles because we know that together we will find our way out of the cities and the crystalline dunes. We experience respect from our sisters. We know who we are because our sisters tell us. Great Dreamer knows who she is because she sees herself in us.

We, all of us, are women of faith. We have faith in our dreaming and our sacred circles. Otherwise we would not have survived the last five thousand years! We rest in the arms of grace. We will become wild, full of life, in love with life, and at peace with ourselves, simply by dreaming the dream and giving the gift.

In some tribal traditions, women beaded and sewed their dreaming onto their clothes. That way, when a woman walked into a tipi or a room, she didn't need to explain herself. The woman's story was on her clothing. I love that image. I have always longed to be so clear that anyone could simply look at me and know my story.

Helen, a quilter, told the circle of a dream that reminded me of wearing the dream. I think Helen found her dream slightly concerning until the circle members spoke to her of the dream's impact.

Entity in the Bathroom

Helen

☽ in ♑

MOON IN CAPRICORN

I go into a little cottage that I own and that has been vacant for several months. I am cleaning it up. There is a small basket that is moving around in the bathtub. I guess that there is a kitten inside and look in, only to discover that it is empty.

The basket is still moving. I run water into it and throw a burning tissue into it, but it continues to move around. I become frightened.

Connie and the rest of the dream group come over but not to share dreams. We are preparing for some event. I keep saying that there is an "entity" in the bathroom, as it continues to worry and scare me, but Connie and the rest of the women seem unconcerned. Connie gives everyone a small teaspoon of a homeopathic medicine and a spool of thread to weave into the front of a shirt as a decoration. I begin to feel high and do the weaving effortlessly. I realize that I am no longer worried about the "entity."

According to our circle, Helen's concern over the moving "entity" that she could not see signifies the pattern of fear we all experience when we are alone or believe we are alone. The "entity" withstood the test of fire and water and lived in the woven basket, the woman's container. Helen's "entity" was the dreaming self who must sometimes alert the dreamer to begin participating in dream work. The circle didn't find Helen's wake-up call alarming or even surprising. The woman's work—weaving the dream—is alive, vibrant, energetic, and enduring. A woman's need to weave the dream will survive any and all attempts to kill it. As Helen's experience shows, when dream work is done together, it is elating and calming.

Ending this book is as difficult as starting it and writing it were. There is no end. Dreaming the dream is the eternal process of the woman. Giving the gift and bestowing life is a woman's expression. How can that end? Circles never end.

The sacred circle work calls us home. The lines of light in our bellies cannot stay hidden any longer. We are crawling out of caves, cracks, gullies, and holes. We are ready to give the gift and live the dream. Our ancestors were clever to stash memory in our wombs. The plan has worked—the memories are awakened. We are rejoicing! We are dreaming. We *are* the dream.

NO END

APPENDIX

HONORING MY TEACHERS

*I*t goes without saying that my husband and children are my most important teachers. Because they love me so thoroughly and so authentically, I am able to walk a path of love. To Vic, Sara, Ben, and Lauren, I give my deepest spiritual, emotional, mental, and physical adoration.

The following people are other teachers who have loved me, taught me, nurtured me, and pushed me. Of course, my words are superficial compared to the energies and states of consciousness they have given me. Descriptions of what my teachers have done for me defy possibility, but I must try. My love for my teachers and my honoring of them is too deep to ignore.

BEAUTIFUL PAINTED ARROW is the medicine name for a remarkable modern-day mystic, Joseph Rael. He is Southern Ute and Picuris by genetics, but he is a citizen of the world by birthright. His method of teaching is quiet, demure, and humble. His effect is shattering, transformative, and unnameable. The hours I have spent walking, talking, praying, chanting, and in ceremony with him count among the most important moments of my life. He reminded me of my medicine. He evoked my power and authenticity. He taught me to "fall more and more in love with life every day." Thank you, Joseph. May you receive the beauty in life that you have brought to mine.

MINISA CRUMBO-HALSEY introduced me to the woman's way. She reminded me to honor my moon time, and she held the deer rattle that sent me into the vision of the dreaming fibers. She gave without taking. I remember one day I called to see if I could come see her, and she said, "Sure, come on up. I'm just wallowing in domestic bliss! You may as well join me." When I arrived, she was ironing. "Domestic bliss? This is your idea of domestic bliss?" She assured me that perspective is the key to life. Minisa never accepted me as a student, even though I asked and pleaded. Yet she gave me some of life's deepest teachings. Minisa reminded me to be the woman I am.

JAMIE SAMS, Coyote Trickster Makes Me Laugh Woman, is more passionately alive than any person I have ever met. I have never taken a seminar or class from Jamie, sat in ceremony with her, or paid her for anything she has taught me. And yet she has altered my life profoundly. Her presence in my life does not require telephone lines, definition, or proximity. We are sisters in the dream. We know each other intimately, because we know the work of dreaming. Her book, *Dancing the Dream*, is a veritable manifesto for the initiation process of dreamers. Thank you, Jamie Sams, for your friendship, your love, your advice, your unconditional presence, your wisdom, your passion, and your jokes.

MALIDOMA SOME has been the most consistent and faithful of my teachers. He is always there, always in tune, and always ready. Whether I need a radical intervention ritual or my husband and son are looking for a companion to take to a Laker game, Malidoma's there. His teachings plunge more deeply than I can verbalize, because they are sourced in beginningness and deep beingness. They are from our ancient ancestors, our African roots, and our earliest human selves. He is the most educated and articulate man I know; he is the most indigenous man I know. He is my brother, my father, my teacher, and my other. This life will not afford me time to reciprocate Malidoma's gifts to me.

SOBONFU SOME, half my age and twice my wisdom, lives without guilt and loves without reservation. She is simultaneously untarnished by Western modernity and totally sophisticated. She has not taught me in a traditional way, and yet from Sobonfu I have learned the traditional ways. She has taught me the concept of *village*. She counsels me in my most important life role: mothering. She reminds me of what has integral meaning and what has projection. She never judges, and yet she never lets me—or Malidoma—get by with our own judgments. Sobonfu is a miracle woman. How could I have been so fortunate to meet and be loved by one such as you?

HEATHER VALENCIA comes last, not because of importance but because of alphabetical imperative. Heather is almost too magical to describe. She is the Dream Weave embodied. She is power dancing through form. Heather is a miracle expressed through the body of a woman. Since the day we met, she has been unbendingly faithful in her generosity and dedication to me. Heather has voluntarily come to life to be our loving sister. She dreams the world and lives in the world. She gives the teachings and lives the teachings. Heather sees life for what it could be and accepts life for what it is. She taught me the ancient form of dream circle and reminded me that women are sisters, not competitors. She stirred my bone-deep memories of ancient temple rites. Heather's tinkling laugh transforms my consciousness and delivers me to the lap of my highest self. Heather, I love you.

DREAM CIRCLE READING LIST

Dreaming Guides

Being-in-Dreaming: An Initiation into the Sorcerer's World. Florinda Donner. San Francisco: HarperSanFrancisco, 1992.

Dancing the Dream. Jamie Sams.* San Francisco: HarperSan-Francisco, 1998.

Dreamgates: An Explorer's Guide to Worlds of Soul, Imagination, and Life Beyond Death. Robert Moss. New York: Crown Publishing Group, 1998.

Dreamwork for the Soul: A Spiritual Guide to Dream Interpretation. Rosemary Ellen Guiley. New York: Berkley Publishing, 1998.

In the Company of Friends: Dreamwork within a Sufi Group. Llewellyn Vaughan-Lee.* Inverness, Calif.: The Golden Sufi Center, 1994.

Journey to Ixtlan. Carlos Castaneda.* New York: Simon & Schuster Trade, 1991.

The Kin of Ata Are Waiting for You. Dorothy Bryant. New York: Random House, 1976.

Queen of Dreams: The Story of a Yaqui Dreaming Woman. Heather Valencia and Rully Kentz. New York: Simon & Schuster Trade, 1993. Web site: www.queenofdreams.com.

The Sorcerer's Crossing: A Woman's Journey. Taisha Abelar. New York: Viking Penguin, 1993.

The Tibetan Yogas of Dream and Sleep. Tenzin Wangyal Rinpoche. Ithaca, N.Y.: Snow Lion Publications, 1998.

Science and Physics

The Dream of the Earth. Thomas Berry.* San Francisco: Sierra Club Books, 1988.

The Eagle's Quest: A Physicist Finds the Scientific Truth at the Heart of the Shamanic World. Fred Alan Wolf.* New York: Simon & Schuster Trade, Touchstone, 1992.

Stalking the Wild Pendulum: On the Mechanics of Consciousness. Itzhak Bentov. Rochester, Vt.: Inner Traditions International, 1988.

The Tao of Physics: An Exploration of the Parallels between Modern Physics and Eastern Mysticism. Fritjof Capra.* Boston: Shambhala, 1991.

The Universe Is a Green Dragon: A Cosmic Creation Story. Brian Swimme.* Santa Fe, N.M.: Bear & Co., 1984.

The Universe Story: From the Promordial Flaring Forth to the Ecozoic Era—A Celebration of the Unfolding of the Cosmos. Brian Swimme and Thomas Berry. San Francisco: HarperSanFrancisco, 1994.

Consciousness Guides

Being and Vibration. Joseph Rael.* Tulsa, Okla.: Council Oak Books, 1993.

Joseph Rael (Beautiful Painted Arrow). A series of videotapes of lectures by Joseph Rael produced by Val Mijailovic and Madeleine Randall. Van Nuys, Calif.: Exclusive Pictures/Heaven Fire Productions, 1995. Web site: www.exclusivepictures.com.

Minding the Temple of the Soul: Balancing Body, Mind and Spirit through Traditional Jewish Prayer, Movement and Meditation. Tamar Frankiel and Judy Greenfeld. Woodstock, Vt.: Jewish Lights Publishing, 1997. Also on videotape produced by Val Mijailovic and Madeleine Randall. Web site: www.exclusivepictures.com.

Of Water and the Spirit: Ritual, Magic and Initiation in the Life of an African Shaman. Malidoma P. Some.* New York: Viking Penguin, 1995.

The Spirit of Intimacy: Ancient Teachings in the Ways of Relationships. Sobonfu E. Some. Berkeley, Calif.: Berkeley Hills Books, 1997.

The Starseed Transmissions. Ken Carey.* San Francisco: HarperSanFrancisco, 1991.

Voices of the Old Ones. A videotape of a lecture by Heather Valencia produced by Val Mijailovic and Madeleine Randall. Van Nuys, Calif.: Exclusive Pictures/Heaven Fire Productions, 1998. Web site: www.exclusivepictures.com.

Walking between the Worlds: The Science of Compassion. Gregg Braden. Bellevue, Wash.: Radio Bookstore Press, 1997.

Women Who Run with the Wolves: Myths and Stories of the Wild Woman Archetype. Clarissa Pinkola Estes. New York: Ballantine, 1992.

Goddess Culture

The Chalice and the Blade: Our History, Our Future. Riane T. Eisler. San Francisco: HarperSanFrancisco, 1988.

The Mists of Avalon. Marion Zimmer Bradley.* New York: Ballantine, 1985.

When God Was a Woman. Merlin Stone. San Diego: Harcourt Brace, Harvest, 1978.

Native American Teachings

Changing Woman and Her Sisters. Sheila Moon. San Francisco: Guild for Psychological Studies Publishing House, 1985.

Daughters of Copper Woman. Anne Cameron.* Milford, Conn.: LPC/InBook, 1981.

Not for Innocent Ears: Spiritual Traditions of a Desert Cahuilla Medicine Woman. Ruby Modesto and Guy Mount. Cottonwood, Calif.: Sweetlight Books, 1986.

The Sacred Hoop: Recovering the Feminine in American Indian Traditions. Paula Gunn Allen. Boston: Beacon Press, 1992.

Song of Heyoehkah. Hyemeyohsts Storm.* New York: Ballantine, 1983.

The Thirteen Original Clan Mothers: Your Sacred Path to Discovering the Gifts, Talents, and Abilities of the Feminine through the Ancient Teachings of the Sisterhood. Jamie Sams.* San Francisco: HarperSanFrancisco, 1994.

Voices of Our Ancestors: Cherokee Teachings from the Wisdom Fire. Dhyani Ywahoo. Boston: Shambhala, 1987.

Other

The Heroine's Journey: Woman's Quest for Wholeness. Maureen Murdoch. Boston: Shambhala, 1990.

Making the Gods Work for You: The Astrological Language of the Psyche. Caroline W. Casey. New York: Harmony Books, 1998.

The Return of Merlin. Deepak Chopra. New York: Harmony Books, 1995.

Sea Priestess. Dion Fortune.* York Beach, Maine: Samuel Weiser, 1972.

The Spiral Dance: A Rebirth of the Ancient Religion of the Great Goddess. Starhawk.* New York: HarperCollins, 1989.

*Or anything else by that author.

HEATHER'S DREAM PILLOW

*T*he following is a magical recipe for a dream pillow shared by Heather Valencia. Make a very small (4″ × 4″) pillow out of any fabric you like. Put approximately equal parts of each of the following raw herbs inside. Keep the pillow near your nose and eyes when you are sleeping. It will help bring power to your dreams, and it will help you remember them!

Mugwort　　　Beloved of Elfin-kind. Attunes you to the etheric electronic realms.

Wormwood　　Helps you to ingest Prana. Opens the third eye. Helps you to go between worlds.

Blue vervain　The blue color affects the hypothalamus and pituitary glands, stimulating creativity and wisdom.

Hyssop　　　The Great Protector. Prevents nightmares.

Mandrake　　The Magician's Root. Empowers you to bring what you acquire in the dream realm into material reality. "Protector" safeguards against evil. Helps you to remember dreams.

Chapparal	A depossessor. Invokes the hierarchy of the nature spirits for the manifestation of power.
Yarrow	Grandmother Herb. Beloved by the old and wise ancient Chinese and American Indians. Good for doing research. Places one in tune with the Akashic records, the energetically recorded account of all that has ever been.
Catnip	Balances the electric and etheric body by, on the physical plane, relieving congestion affecting the nerves.
Cumin	Possesses the power of retention. Evokes the good fellowship of the "nature spirits."
Buchu leaves	Reveals the future. Stimulates creative imagery.
Rock salt	A natural crystal formation. Adds clarity and facilitates dreaming in color.

OTHER BOOKS FROM BEYOND WORDS PUBLISHING, INC.

HEALING YOUR RIFT WITH GOD
A Guide to Spiritual Renewal and Ultimate Healing
Author: Paul R. Sibcy
$14.95, softcover

God, says Paul Sibcy, is everything that is. All of us—faithful seekers or otherwise—have some area of confusion, hurt, or denial around this word, or our personal concept of God, that keeps us from a full expression of our spirituality. *Healing Your Rift with God* is a guidebook for finding our own personal rifts with God and healing them. Sibcy explains the nature of a spiritual rift, how this wound can impair our lives, and how such a wound may be healed by the earnest seeker, with or without help from a counselor or teacher. *Healing Your Rift with God* will also assist those in the helping professions who wish to facilitate what the author calls ultimate healing. The book includes many personal stories from the author's life, teaching, and counseling work, and its warm narrative tone creates an intimate author—reader relationship that inspires the healing process.

DIVINE INTERVENTION
A Journey from Chaos to Clarity
Author: Susan Anderson; Foreword: David Lukoff, Ph.D.;
Afterword: Emma Bragdon, Ph.D.
$13.95, softcover

Divine Intervention is a powerfully written and engaging story of spiritual transformation. Susan Anderson's journey from chaos to clarity provides hope and inspiration for anyone facing the challenge of a major crisis or life change. Susan's spiritual emergency causes her to reconnect with her true self and experience an authentic sense of fulfillment and joy that could only be created by a Divine Intervention. Having received rave reviews from doctors, spiritual leaders, and lay readers, this book is a treasure of insight and wisdom that will empower women and men to take charge of their lives. For those wanting to help anyone in a spiritual emergency, also included is a guide and resource directory by Emma Bragdon, Ph.D., author of *Sourcebook for Helping People in Spiritual Emergency*.

HOW MUCH JOY CAN YOU STAND?
How to Push Past Your Fears and Create Your Dreams
Author: Suzanne Falter-Barns
$12.95, softcover

This is the little book of wisdom you've been looking for to steer you back on the path of your dreams. In fresh, funny language, *How Much Joy Can You Stand?* demystifies the creative process and gives you the inspirational kick in the pants you've been waiting for. Inside is all the reassurance and encouragement you need to get going and keep going. Stories, anecdotes, and the author's own hard-won wisdom tell the simple truth about creating your dream—that it's not as hard as you think, and you do, indeed, know exactly what you need to know. Find out where to find inspiration, how to handle rejection, whether talent really matters, and how to stick with your work even in the face of couch-potato attacks and complete creative meltdown. Hands-on exercises follow each short, pungent chapter to put you back on track toward achieving your goals. A One Spirit Book Club selection.

THE GREAT WING

A Parable

Author: Louis A. Tartaglia, M.D.

Foreword: Father Angelo Scolozzi

$14.95, hardcover

The Great Wing transforms the timeless miracle of the migration of a flock of geese into a parable for the modern age. It recounts a young goose's own reluctant but steady transformation from gangly fledgling to Grand Goose and his triumph over the turmoils of his soul and the buffeting of a mighty Atlantic storm. In *The Great Wing*, our potential as individuals is affirmed, as is the power of group prayer, or the "Flock Mind." As we make the journey with this goose and his flock, we rediscover that we tie our own potential into the power of the common good by way of attributes such as honesty, hope, courage, trust, perseverance, spirituality, and service. The young goose's trials and tribulations, as well as his triumph, are our own.

A LIFE WORTH LIVING

Recording Your Values, Memories, Goals, and Dreams

Author: Jerry Hawley

$19.95, hardcover

To provide a record of what each of us has done and where we are going, we created *A Life Worth Living*. The book is a living legacy for families to share for generations, and it includes pockets for mementos, blank pages to write affirmations, lots of questions for reflection, and an envelope for special treasures. Like Jimmy Stewart in the movie *It's a Wonderful Life*, few of us realize how our lives impact the people around us. Few of us record the details of our lives so that our children and grandchildren can know who we are, what has made our lives unique, who our friends are, what we have accomplished, and who touched our lives in memorable ways. Imagine the joy of discovering fascinating things about the lives of your parents and grandparents when you read what they have written in *A Life Worth Living*.

PRIDE AND JOY
The Lives and Passions of Women Without Children
Author: Terri Casey
$14.95, softcover

Pride and Joy is an enlightening collection of first-person interviews with twenty-five women who have decided not to have children. This book shatters the stereotypes that surround voluntarily childless women—that they are self-centered, immature, workaholic, unfeminine, materialistic, child-hating, cold, or neurotic. Diversity is a strong suit of this book. The narrators range in age from twenty-six-year-old Sarah Klein, who teaches second grade in an inner-city public school, to eighty-two-year-old Ruby Burton, a retired court reporter who grew up in a mining camp. The women talk about their family histories, intimate relationships, self-images, creative outlets, fears, ambitions, dreams, and connections to the next generation. Even though these women are not mothers, many voluntarily childless women help to raise and sometimes rescue the next generation while retaining the personal freedom they find so integral to their identities.

ANIMAL TALK
Interspecies Telepathic Communication
Author: Penelope Smith
$14.95, softcover

If your animal could speak, what would it say? In *Animal Talk*, Penelope Smith presents effective telepathic communication techniques that can dramatically transform people's relationships with animals on all levels. Her insightful book explains how to solve behavior problems, how to figure out where your animal hurts, how to discover animals' likes and dislikes, and why they do the things they do. Without resorting to magic tricks or wishful thinking, *Animal Talk* teaches you how to open the door to your animal friends' hearts and minds. An entire chapter of this illuminating book is devoted to teaching people how to develop mind-to-mind communication with animals. *Animal Talk* also explores the following topics: freedom, control, and obedience; understanding behavior from an animal's point of view; how to handle upsets between animals; tips on nutrition for healthier pets; and the special relationship between animals and children. There is even a section on how to communicate with fleas and other insects!

WHEN ANIMALS SPEAK
Advanced Interspecies Communication
Author: Penelope Smith; Foreword: Michael J.Roads
$14.95, softcover

In her first book, *Animal Talk*, Penelope Smith confirmed what many people had hoped was true—that we can communicate with our animal friends. *When Animals Speak* takes us to a deeper level as life-changing revelations are communicated directly from the animals. You will discover who animals say they truly are; how they feel about humans and life on earth; how they choose their paths in life and death; what their spiritual understanding and purposes are; and how they can be our teachers, helping us heal ourselves and guiding us back to wholeness. By regaining the language understood by all species, you will laugh and cry as you experience the animals' refreshing, moving, and sometimes startling points of view. *When Animals Speak* will become a treasured key to your own intuitive connection with the rest of creation.

KINSHIP WITH THE ANIMALS
Editors: Michael Tobias and Kate Solisti-Mattelon
$15.95, softcover

Contributors to *Kinship with the Animals* represent a myriad of countries and traditions. From Jane Goodall illustrating the emergence of her lifelong devotion to animals to Linda Tellington-Jones describing her experiences communicating with animals through touch, the thirty-three stories in *Kinship with the Animals* deconstruct traditional notions of animals by offering a new and insightful vision of animals as conscious beings capable of deep feelings and sophisticated thoughts. The editors have deliberately sought stories that present diverse views of animal awareness and communication.

LOVE SWEETER LOVE
Creating Relationships of Simplicity and Spirit
Author: Jann Mitchell; Foreword: Susan Jeffers
$12.95, softcover

How do we find the time to nurture relationships with the people we love? By simplifying. And *Love Sweeter Love* teaches us how to decide who and what is most important, how to work together as a couple, and how to savor life's sweetest moments. Mitchell has warm, practical, easy-to-understand advice for everyone—young, mature, single, married, or divorced—interested in creating simple, sacred time for love.

HOME SWEETER HOME
Creating a Haven of Simplicity and Spirit
Author: Jann Mitchell; Foreword: Jack Canfield
$12.95, softcover

We search the world for spirituality and peace—only to discover that happiness and satisfaction are not found "out there" in the world but right here in our houses and in our hearts. Award-winning journalist and author Jann Mitchell offers creative insights and suggestions for making our home life more nurturing, spiritual, and rewarding for ourselves, our families, and our friends.

RITES OF PASSAGE
Celebrating Life's Changes
Authors: Kathleen Wall, Ph.D., and Gary Ferguson
$12.95, softcover

Every major transition in our lives—be it marriage, high-school graduation, the death of a parent or spouse, or the last child leaving home—brings with it opportunities for growth and self-actualization and for repositioning ourselves in the world. Personal ritual—the focus of *Rites of Passage*—allows us to use the energy held within the anxiety of change to nourish the new person that is forever struggling to be born. *Rites of Passage* begins by explaining to readers that human growth is not linear, as many of us assume, but rather occurs in a five-part cycle. After sharing the patterns of transition, the authors then show the reader how ritual can help him or her move through these specific life changes: work and career, intimate relationships, friends, divorce, changes within the family, adolescence, issues in the last half of life, and personal loss.

CREATE YOUR OWN LOVE STORY
The Art of Lasting Relationships
Author: David W. McMillan, Ph.D.; Foreword: John Gray
$21.95, hardcover; $14.95, softcover

Create Your Own Love Story breaks new ground in the crowded and popular field of relationship self-help guides. *Create Your Own Love Story* is based on a four-part model—Spirit, Trust, Trade, and Art—derived from McMillan's twenty years' work in community theory and clinical psychology. Each of these four elements is divided into short, highly readable chapters that include both touching and hilarious examples from real marriages, brief exercises based on visualization and journal writing that are effective whether used by one or both partners, and dialogues readers can have with themselves and/or their partners. This book shows readers how they can use their own energy and initiative, with McMillan's help, to make their marriage stronger, more enduring, and more soul-satisfying.

THE INTUITIVE WAY
A Guide to Living from Inner Wisdom
Author: Penney Peirce; Foreword: Carol Adrienne
$16.95, softcover

When intuition is in full bloom, life takes on a magical, effortless quality; your world is suddenly full of synchronicities, creative insights, and abundant knowledge just for the asking. *The Intuitive Way* shows you how to enter that state of perceptual aliveness and integrate it into daily life to achieve greater natural flow through an easy-to-understand, ten-step course. Author Penney Peirce synthesizes teachings from psychology, East-West philosophy, religion, metaphysics, and business. In simple and direct language, Peirce describes the intuitive process as a new way of life and demonstrates many practical applications from speeding decision-making to expanding personal growth. Whether you're just beginning to search for a richer, fuller life experience or are looking for more subtle, sophisticated insights about your spiritual path, *The Intuitive Way* will be your companion as you progress through the stages of intuition development.

NURTURING SPIRITUALITY IN CHILDREN
Author: Peggy J. Jenkins, Ph.D.
$10.95, softcover

Children who develop a healthy balance of mind and spirit enter adulthood with high self-esteem, better able to respond to life's challenges. Many parents wish to heighten their children's spiritual awareness but have been unable to find good resources. *Nurturing Spirituality in Children* offers scores of simple lessons that parents can teach to their children in less than ten minutes at a time.

EMBRACING THE GODDESS WITHIN
A Creative Guide for Women
Author: Kris Waldherr
$17.95, hardcover

Embracing the Goddess Within continues the tradition of Kris Waldherr's best-selling *The Book of Goddesses*. Exquisite, magical, and joyous, this glowing book resonates with the energy that for thousands of years has been summed up in the word *goddess*. *Embracing the Goddess Within* is divided into six sections that mirror the eternal feminine rites of passage: Beginnings, Love, Motherhood, Creativity, Strength, and Transformations. Each section contains a selection of goddesses for that particular stage or interest of a woman's life, giving her guidance for whatever challenge she faces. Each goddess is presented in a lyrical accounting of her myth accompanied by a beautiful illustration and simple ritual designed to invoke her spirit and power. Romantic, visually stunning, and as fun as it is practical, *Embracing the Goddess Within* is an essential addition to the personal library of all twenty-first-century goddesses.

SACRED FLOWERS
Creating a Heavenly Garden
Author: Roni Jay
$14.95, hardcover

For thousands of years the magical qualities of flowers have been held sacred by traditions around the world: the lily to the Christian church, the lotus to Asian cultures, the rose to both the Christian and Muslim faiths. *Sacred Flowers* explores the special powers attributed to a fragrant collection of flora. You will discover which flower placed under a pillow can give romantic dreams, which flowering herb will help restore a friendship, which flower pinned to your clothing will protect you, which blossom is an aid to astral projection and prophecy, and which flower will give you the courage to realize your dreams. *Sacred Flowers* reveals the healing properties of flowers for the mind, body, and spirit. You can draw upon this wealth of ancient lore to explore the medicinal or inspirational effects of a fragrance, and the book will help you to design and create a mystical and spiritual paradise in your own yard or patio.

KNOW YOUR TRUTH, SPEAK YOUR TRUTH, LIVE YOUR TRUTH

Author: Eileen R. Hannegan, M.S.

$12.95, softcover

Know Your Truth, Speak Your Truth, Live Your Truth is a transformational guide for those seeking truth and authenticity in their personal and professional lives. This book provides inspiration, encouragement, and practical steps on the road to discovering and living one's own truth. *Know Your Truth, Speak Your Truth, Live Your Truth* is filled with illustrative stories as well as exercises, affirmations, and questions for reflection that will enhance your personal and spiritual growth and light the way to owning, asserting, and honoring the power of the truth within.

To order or to request a catalog, contact

Beyond Words Publishing, Inc.
20827 N.W. Cornell Road, Suite 500
Hillsboro, OR 97124-9808
503-531-8700 or 1-800-284-9673

You can also visit our Web site at www.beyondword.com
or e-mail us at info@beyondword.com.

BEYOND WORDS PUBLISHING, INC.

Our Corporate Mission:

Inspire to Integrity

Our Declared Values:

We give to all of life as life has given to us.

We honor all relationships.

Trust and stewardship are integral to fulfilling dreams.

Collaboration is essential to create miracles.

Creativity and aesthetics nourish the soul.

Unlimited thinking is fundamental.

Living your passion is vital.

Joy and humor open our hearts to growth.

It is important to remind ourselves of love.